KU-273-474

The most valuable thing in the world could be said not to exist.

An idea has no substance.

And yet it is the root of your personal contribution to the world, to your business, to your art, to your customer and to your happiness.

Your thoughts and ideas, which are the reason people want to employ you, buy from you and simply be with you are nothing more than the product of infinitesimally small electronic pulses.

Like the foam of a distant wave that crests and then melts back into the sea your thoughts are fleeting, beautiful and then gone.

When you stand on a cliff and scan an energetic sea you can glimpse hundreds of these 'white horses'.

Each is unique, just as your thoughts are unique to you. Your ideas are built on the accumulated experience of all that you have experienced in your long life, just as a wave has travelled the furthest deep ocean before it briefly breaks, bursts and blends back to blue.

These are your unique creations and they can change your life.

They can change the way other people – and even the universe – interact with you.

And they can change your world; how you perceive it, how it sees you and how you and everything else rub along together.

Without the right habits of mind, trying to generate and capture these thoughts is like trying to catch a wave with a butterfly net.

Here are nine ways to ride your own white horse back to shore.

'If I had a view like this to look down on every day, I would have the energy and inspiration to conquer the world.

The trouble is, when you most need such a view, no-one gives it to you'

Jennifer Egan, A Visit from the Goon Squad

THE
LITTLE BOOK
OF THINKING
BIG

Aim higher and go further than
you ever thought possible

Richard Newton

CAPSTONE
A Wiley Brand

9 HABITS OF

THINKING BIG

'You get what anybody gets
– you get a lifetime.'

Neil Gaiman, *The Sandman*

WHITE HORSE WHISPERING

Not long ago you knew what to expect.

You were born in the town or village where you would die and in between those two events you would occupy yourself in much the same way as your parents did.

You'd inherit the same work, tools, beliefs and ambition.

The world around you advanced slowly and incrementally and your future looked like your past.

You only had to fire up your imagination the merest bit to overshoot reality by a distance.

So, in those days thinking big was for fairy tales.

Fast forward to right now, to this instant as your eyes pass over these words, and all that has changed profoundly.

Today, imagination is no longer for fairy tales. Today your unshackled imagination is the truest designer of your future.

The new certainty is that everything changes, anything is possible and whatever you can imagine is probably on the cusp of being made real tomorrow and obsolete soon after.

So fast is the world transforming that only if you think wildly and recklessly will you even keep up with what's coming down the road. Merely to keep up you must overshoot like an archer aims ahead of a moving object.

To go further, if you want to seize control and shape your future the requirement is clearer still: you must unshackle your imagination expand your ambition, sweep past boundaries and think always, ever bigger.

Because the bottom line is this, your imagination is now the limiting factor of your life. In the world of anything-is-possible the outer limits of thinking big are the barriers of your life.

Make them small and that is the life you will have. Throw them far and then never stop extending them and you shall never limit yourself.

You may not achieve the ends of your imagination and ambition. But you certainly will not go past it.

Like anything that can change your life, thinking big takes practice. And most people have skipped the habit for years.

Thinking big is all too often replaced by the narrow thinking that the pressures of everyday life throw at us. These pressures are real and are not lightly dismissed. But the narrowness of thinking won't change your world like your white horses of inspiration, insight and ambition.

People construct cages for themselves. Iron bars of self-doubt and not-smart-enough here, the possibility of failure there, the approval of the crowd, money worries and so on. This is how you build it.

Maybe, as you climb inside you say: this is only for a while. I will run free as soon as I am done with these worries.

And time ticks. And as the minute hand whirls, the habits of thinking-your-life-bigger get lost by the relentless head-down tackling-of-tasks that must be dealt with.

The danger for you is that this becomes a life of mere existence.

An expert on zoos recently said something about the lives of imprisoned animals and it is a true statement for we humans too:

'A tally of years lived and calorically balanced meals eaten doesn't account for quality of life or the pleasure that can come from making one's own decisions.'

Thinking big isn't a one off exercise.

It's a way of being. It is about always seeing the world big and broad and, as they say in *The Simpsons*, it's about 'embiggening' your part of it.

The habits of thinking big are easy to use and with practice become always at hand.

Even the simple matter of identifying what these habits are and labelling them will help you notice what you're doing, what you're not doing and when you should or shouldn't be doing it. You'll become more sensitive to when you're creeping back into the cage and, more importantly, relish those ever more frequent times when you are making your life potential greater.

In the end this is about consciously and deliberately tweaking your attitude to fully achieve your unique, here-for-one-lifetime-only potential.

Just as the experience of knowing the name of an actor but being unable to remember it is familiar to all of us, so is the feeling that the wisp of a great idea or a higher understanding is just shimmering out of reach. These are our white horses. This is your potential.

Bringing them home begins with the first habit.

Swim, don't float.

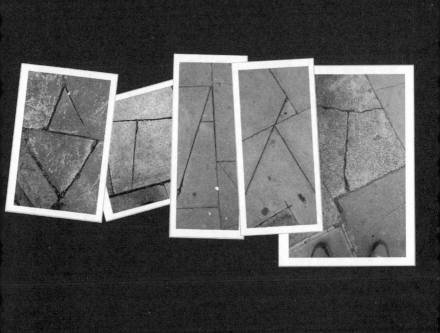

'If you take two steps towards God,' he used to tell me, 'God runs to you!'

Yann Martel, *Life of Pi*

SWIM DON'T FLOAT

Life lessons from a sea squirt

Sea squirts begin life looking much like a regular tadpole. Hatched from an egg they swim around the ocean looking for nutrients and a place to settle.

For so long as the sea squirt is swimming with purpose through the water, feeding and looking for a rock to perch on, it uses its brain. Upon finding a suitable rock or ship wreck it attaches itself. It will never move again.

Thereafter it is not the sea squirt that directs itself. The ocean moves as it will and if this should happen to bring nourishment to the sea squirt then so be it.

The sea squirt is reactive. It is not a motive force in its own life. It cannot control its fate.

Having no further need for it, the sea squirt consumes its brain.

Your human brain is a greedy pig. It weighs just 1/50 of your total body weight yet consumes 1/5 of your daily energy. To send a solitary signal a brain cell uses as much energy as a muscle cell in your leg uses during an entire marathon.

The first lesson of the sea squirt is this: if you're not going to use it; eat it.

Otherwise you're wasting energy.

The sea squirt gets a burst of growth energy when it consumes its rudimentary brain and nerve cells.

This energy helps it to metamorphose into something that looks like an avant-garde hand bag.

THE FIRST LESSON OF THE SEA SQUIRT

USE IT

OR

EAT IT

HANDBAG
de
SEA
SQUIRT

Energy begets energy

If you choose to keep your brain it will use a lot of energy. But the energy it consumes is nothing compared to its output; which can do anything from raising your mood to raising a flag on the moon.

Maximizing that output is the purpose of this book.

You came into this world bursting with wonder, imagination, curiosity, the urge to be creative and, as any crawling wanna-walk baby will show you, you were born with unflinching and boundless ambition.

Over the course of the days and weeks and years these natural-born traits rub up against the real world and shape your fascinating, compelling essence. Your core.

You develop tastes, interests, pleasures, aversions, ambitions and dreams.

But these traits also take a pounding from real world pressures like work life, fear of being laughed at, social media judgement, nine-to-five drudgery, financial pressure and the strong urge to fit in, conform, and follow instructions or routines.

And under this siege sometimes you yield and smother your white horses; you lose track of your imaginative spark, your dreams and your daring ambition.

But they're still there. You can realize your extraordinary potential and expand your horizons at any stage of life.

The simple truth of this book is that where you direct your mind you move your life.

> 'The greatest discovery of
> my generation is that human beings
> can alter their lives by altering their
> attitude of mind...
> If you change your mind, you
> can change your life.'
>
> *William James*

Any mind will do

Thinking bigger doesn't require you to bring a certificate of astrophysics
or etch a philosopher's frown onto your forehead. You only need to
commit to using the energy-hungry grey cells in your cranium.

We are not all superstar scientists, businessmen, artists or chefs.
But we can all reach greater heights with the tools that we have.

Each of us has inside us an original view of the world. To open
these windows you must activate your mind and your imagination.

You have a short time left to you. Your wave left a distant shore
many years ago.

The sooner you get into the right frame of mind the further you
will see and the more you will achieve in every aspect of your life.

Hustle.

The trouble with thinking is that it's not much to look at.

Everything else about it is capital B-Big.

Thinking bigger will produce better decisions, better ideas, increased creativity, more understanding, greater insight, better judgement, more resilience and more fortitude. It will unleash your imagination and harness your intuition.

And these, the products of thinking bigger, impact positively wherever you direct your grey matter.

This might be the office environment, career trajectory, home life, relationships, art (your own and others'), entrepreneurial achievement, sports training, marvelling at the wonders of the universe or starting smaller and just learning to cope with everyday life.

That's the prize.

So let's start.

Failing to gasp in awe at
the immensity of your
potential is like bricking up
your windows.

Lift your gaze from trivia;
imagine without limits,
let loose your dreams, see
the full universe of your
possibility.

Then open the window
and climb out.

W.A.I.T.

WHAT AM I THINKING ?

Here's the thing.

There isn't a secret door, a magic bullet, an Elvish oath, or a golden ticket.

There's you.

That's all.

And nothing else is required. You are your own key.

There is no ambition, courage or imagination you need which isn't already inside you. This is about bringing it roaring to the surface.

To make progress in all your daily battles the starting point is resetting how you choose to think all day.

This is the platform from which all your small victories and big success will sputter and then gush forth. This may seem abstract. Don't be fooled. This is the only route to unleashing your ideas, building on your life's experiences and changing your world.

Where you direct your mind's awesome potential will steer and shape your life.

'Life', said Ralph Waldo Emerson, 'consists of what a man is thinking all day'.

Everything that follows starts from this principle.

Your brain is humming with energy all day long. Whatever it's humming about is what your life is.

What you can do right now, this instant, is begin to exert conscious control over what you are thinking all day.

Get used to thinking **'W.A.I.T.' (What Am I Thinking?)**.

Controlling your thoughts means switching off your mental auto-pilot and the unreflective, unconscious way you react to life's hiccups, tragedies and opportunities.

David Foster Wallace wrote:

> 'Learning how to think really means learning how to exercise some control over how and what you think. It means being conscious and aware enough to choose what you pay attention to and to choose how you construct meaning from experience.'

The important word here is: **choose**. You can allow yourself to be bothered all day long about, let's say, the personal slight that you once suffered or the endless fictional arguments in your head. That's a lot of your energy being buffeted around to the benefit of precisely no-one.

Or you can choose not to.

As you get better at disciplining your thoughts your life gets bigger because you invest more of your life's energy into the activities that increase your happiness and success while putting less energy into the things that don't.

And that is how you create a bigger life.

And ultimately it is how you will surprise yourself by gripping on tight, yodelling wildly and riding a white horse back to shore.

I'm not saying this is easy.

The easy thing, the cruelly easy thing, is not to do this. The easiest thing in the world is to be a brainless sea squirt whose life drifts here and there, but ultimately nowhere, subject to the push and pull of the tide. This is the life of a puppet whose strings are pulled by advertising, hearsay, fears, slogans, bullying, peer pressure, road rage, hunger pangs and sharp flashes of emotional response.

It's actually quite hard to control your thoughts all day long. Even those who were fortunate enough to be taught to think at university, or taught by a religious teacher, a spiritual leader, Mary Poppins or the school of hard knocks sometimes need reminding.

'Thinking is a skill', said Edward de Bono, one of the leading contemporary writers on the way we use our minds. 'It is not intelligence in action'.

Happily it's something you can get better at.

If it's a skill then anyone can improve, just as anyone can get better at playing the piano, public speaking, drawing, boxing, swimming, programming, baking, texting on a smartphone, World of Warcraft and The Sims.

Yes, this takes effort, but it's far from impossible and it's unbelievably important. More than important. It's the foundation for everything you experience. Life, as we have already said (and will repeat many times precisely because it is so important) is what you are thinking.

This is no mere flim-flammery about airy-fairy wish fulfilment. This is hard won practical advice. What could be more practical than to realize that where you focus your mind is where you will focus your time and your energy?

You can think your life bigger. Or smaller.

Before I protest too much, it's time for an example.

The father of gonzo journalism and writer of *Fear & Loathing in Las Vegas* advised a friend:

'... And indeed, that IS the question: whether to float with the tide, or to swim for a goal. It is a choice we must all make consciously or unconsciously at one time in our lives. So few people understand this! Think of any decision you've ever made which had a bearing on your future: I may be wrong, but I don't see how it could have been anything but a choice however indirect— between the two things I've mentioned: the floating or the swimming.'

Massive Monday

In the world of recruitment they call the first working day of the New Year, 'Massive Monday'. The number of people looking for change – a new job, career or life – peaks on Day One of the year.

...Aaaand then it tails off. People begin each year intending to achieve more, to bend the world to their ambitions. The timing, of course, is obvious. It is when the obligatory (for most) holiday from work meets the psychic and emotional milestone of crossing off another year. It means people take time to reflect, pause and breathe. They use their minds and rediscover their boundless ambition, and this brings to the surface an irrefutable conclusion: they insist on change.

...Aaaand then stuff gets in the way. They lose control of what they thought was important. They get caught in the mental fog of to-do lists, money worries, exhaustion and other priorities, and they postpone their dreams. Ambition gets forced to the bottom, the courage to demand change is exhausted by the courage of battling through the headwind of mere existence.

Autopilot takes over. The busyness of life takes over. Real priorities get lost in the noisy small stuff.

The tide pulls them this way and that.

Another 12 months of unfulfilment passes until it cannot be borne any longer.

And Massive Monday comes round again.

This happens every year.

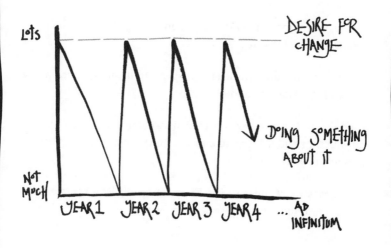

THE BALLAD OF MASSIVE MONDAY

Lots — DESIRE FOR CHANGE

DOING SOMETHING ABOUT IT

Not MUCH

YEAR 1   YEAR 2   YEAR 3   YEAR 4   ... AD INFINITUM

Every year.
This is normal.
This is stupid.

Sea squirts eat their brains.

Life consists of what someone is thinking all day

It takes discipline to maintain focus on the big picture; to keep focused on the big stuff.

But then again, don't the biggest rewards in life pretty much always demand at least some effort?

(By the way, if you know how to achieve change through sitting on your butt and making no effort then, watch out, we all want a passport to your world.)

But as Massive Monday shows, the easiest thing is to operate on autopilot, to move with the eddies of the sea.

> 'The brain is a wonderful organ; it starts working the moment you get up in the morning and does not stop until you get into the office.'
>
> *Robert Frost*

It's very easy to stop thinking

But the costs may be high.

An entire culture once stopped critical, scientific thinking.

Baghdad was the intellectual capital of the world in AD800–1100. It was an open society where people from around the world, with different backgrounds and diverse religions came together to trade, create art and develop science.

During this period Arabian numerals were invented – these are the numerals we use today in place of say Roman Numerals which are rarely used outside the Superbowl.

Two thirds of all the named stars in the universe have Arabian names because they were discovered during this period.

This was the centre of the advancement of the world's knowledge. And then in the twelfth century the religious cleric, Hamid al-Ghazali, declared that mathematics, logic and physics was incompatible with Islam.

And that was that. That was the end of Baghdad's position as the world's leading city of science.

Revelation replaced discovery. Scripture replaced science.

Kurt Vonnegut wrote a novel about the absurdity of the way we live. Actually he wrote quite a few of them. In one, Breakfast of Champions, he described in passing why people might choose to stop using their minds.

'Unusual ideas could make enemies', he explained. This wasn't ideal when people needed all the friends they could get.

'So in the interests of survival, they trained themselves to be agreeing machines instead of thinking machines. All their minds had to do was to discover what other people were thinking, and then they thought that too.'

As a result some characters decided to be 'stupid on purpose'.

But that's fiction. Being stupid on purpose seems like the sort of thing no-one would ever do.

...Aaaand yet people do it all the time to fit in with everyone else.

The phenomenon of being deliberately stupid to fit in with the group is described in The Abilene Paradox. The management expert Jerry B. Harvey described it like this:

> 'On a hot afternoon in Coleman, Texas, the family is comfortably playing dominoes on a porch, until the father-in-law suggests that they take a trip to Abilene [53 miles north] for dinner. The wife says, "Sounds like a great idea." The husband, despite having reservations because the drive is long and hot, thinks that his preferences must be out-of-step with the group and says, "Sounds good to me. I just hope your mother wants to go." The mother-in-law then says, "Of course I want to go. I haven't been to Abilene in a long time."
>
> The drive is hot, dusty, and long. When they arrive at the cafeteria, the food is as bad as the drive. They arrive back home four hours later, exhausted.

One of them dishonestly says, "It was a great trip, wasn't it?" The mother-in-law says that, actually, she would rather have stayed home, but went along since the other three were so enthusiastic. The husband says, "I wasn't delighted to be doing what we were doing. I only went to satisfy the rest of you." The wife says, "I just went along to keep you happy. I would have had to be crazy to want to go out in the heat like that." The father-in-law then says that he only suggested it because he thought the others might be bored.

The group sits back, perplexed that they together decided to take a trip which none of them wanted. They each would have preferred to sit comfortably, but did not admit to it when they still had time to enjoy the afternoon.'

And time, that precious resource, drains away, wasted, whenever we don't use our minds to make the most of it.

And this is the second lesson of the sea squirt:

Either your mind digests life and makes it the best it can be.
Or you sit stationary on the sea bed and life digests your mind.

Burp.

EITHER YOU DIGEST LIFE OR LIFE DIGESTS YOU

The Wild Pigs of the Okefenokee Swamp

A stranger halts his horse and wagon alongside a general store on the fringe of the untamed Okefenokee Swamp.

He calls over: "I'm here to catch pigs."

The locals burst out laughing. "Those wild, dangerous beasts? No chance."
"The most powerful guns won't stop them. Go home."
"I lost my leg escaping the pigs, stranger. Turn around."

"I wanted to buy some corn, actually", he says. And every week he buys more on his way to the swamp.

The hunters scratch their heads, tap their guns and the months pass until one day the stranger says: "Gentlemen, I need help to take 600 pigs to market."

To stunned silence he explains: "First I put some corn on the edge of a clearing. Each week I led the trail closer to the center."

First, the young pigs but eventually even the largest, fiercest pigs could not resist the lure of easy food.

"They stopped fearing me and one yard at a time I built a pen. Eyes on the corn – they never even noticed."

"It's not possible!" gasped the old-timers. "That's not hunting!"

"Oh it is", he said. "And this morning I shut the gate."

This tale, which I first came across in an article written by Steve Washam, is a two sided morality tale. Both sides beg one thing – Use your mind:

1. The stranger challenges old methods of catching pigs and thus triumphs.

2. The pigs cease thinking and fail to see that gradually (and helpfully) they are being fenced in.

'What I represent in fact, what I'm trying like hell to represent every time I go into that hotel room, is myself.'

Maya Angelou (...whose disciplined writing routine famously required that she go into a specific and spartan hotel room to write her books)

'I don't believe in Beatles, I believe in me.'

John Lennon

'So we do not strive to be firemen, we do not strive to be bankers, nor policemen, nor doctors. WE STRIVE TO BE OURSELVES.'

Hunter S. Thompson

CLEAR SOME (HEAD) SPACE

The Sargasso Sea of the mind

We are perverse.

Consider these questions:
Where and what is your white horse?
What does Massive Monday look like for you?
In what direction will you throw the full force and passion of your energy?
What, in other words, is your truly authentic, personal ambition?

To be truly who you are, wise men and women through the ages have all urged one thing:

'Know yourself'.

Easy enough to say. But we are perverse.

With the boundless ocean of imagination to play in – we can imagine the infinity of space, we can mentally time travel back and forth, we can imagine what it's like to be someone else, we can remember the sound of snow squeaking under our skis and the taste of sea water on our lips and yet...

...with all the immensity of potential to explore, we allow our minds to loiter in the Sargasso Sea of mental clutter.

The Sargasso Sea, in the North Atlantic Ocean, is in the middle of four powerful ocean currents that swirl around and create a vortex that gathers in one place all the Ocean's sea weed, plastic bottles, old fishing nets, shopping bags, rubber ducks and other floating crap.

If there's one place you don't want to hang out when you're trying to surface the white horses of your fresh thinking then it's the mental equivalent of the North Atlantic Garbage Patch.

The Sargasso Sea of the mind is full of the opinions of others, the pressure of the work day, hear say, pinging phones, twitter, trolls, prejudices, busyness, fear and biases.

To surface your own potential, to articulate your personal ambition, to 'know yourself' you have to get away from all of this.

Needless to say, because it's the one place where we shouldn't tarry, it is precisely where we linger and mooch.

THE HIGH SEAS OF THINKING BIG

SEA OF PERSPECTIVE

SEA OF TRANQUILITY

CONTEMPLATION TRIANGLE

INSPIRATION STRAITS

OCEAN OF CREATIVITY

VORTEX OF GARBAGE

WHERE THE MIND GETS TRAPPED

Your true north

Screw the sea squirt, screw being stupid on purpose, screw Massive Monday and bricked up windows. You are going to create a bigger life and that means you are going to use it (not eat it).

You will start unlocking your here-for-one-life-time-only potential because you will start using your mind, practice focusing on the big things that matter and project your energy to make that happen.

> Knowing what matters to you enables you to prioritize where you direct your energy.

There's no catch. You simply need clear direction, to know what matters to you. Which means that to be more and to contribute more, you need to create the head space to bring your true self, your true north, to the surface.

Knowing what matters to you enables you to prioritize where you direct your energy. And when you deliberately put your energy in a single direction you generate momentum and then you make progress.

This is true of art, of business, of your emotional state.

Beware the pre-occupation of narrow thinking

It's easy to be occupied all day by unreflective, unconscious thoughts that ricochet around your skull as an advertisement pops up, a smartphone chirrups, someone ahead of you lets in a queue-jumper and the news media hose you with headlines carefully phrased to achieve a state of peak urgency and alarm.

But here's the thing you gotta face. You let this happen. We all do. We allow our brains to be preoccupied by the wrong priorities. We could use our minds to be bigger people, happier people and contribute more to our lives, to the lives of others and to society.

But we can't help getting consumed by emotions and thoughts that don't really matter. And they eat up our time. And life is minutes. And they go by and by.

We get lost in the Sargasso Sea of preoccupation and every 12 months Massive Monday passes by like a carousel and we say D'oh!

For you Massive Monday may not be the job. It may be something else like the dance class, spending more time outdoors, with the family, learning to paint or working on a side project.

What matters is that we all have our own version of Massive Monday which hits us from time to time when we realize we have invested our anxious energy in the wrong priorities.

Getting those priorities right can only happen when you take time out and find some space for reflection. Which is what happens at the turn of another year... just before Massive Monday.

And that means giving your brain time out from the speeding hamster wheel.

I don't know if this is true. I dearly hope it is. To stop bus drivers going too fast and driving recklessly on hazardous Chinese roads the operating companies suspend a big bowl of water next to the driver. This helps them strive for the big picture – like happy, living passengers.

It's an elegant and non-digital way to pre-occupy a driver's mind with something other than road rage, red mist, dreams of F1 racing or fiddling with the radio on a mountainous hair pin bend.

Allowing your mind to stay busy is easy. It's as if the clutter and noise of the garbage vortex is sucking you in with the gravitational pull of an immense black hole. While you try to get on with life, the vortex flashes and winks and pings at you, begging for your precious attention.

'Living is the least important activity of the pre-occupied man', the ancient Greek philosopher Seneca warned his friend. 'Yet there is nothing which is harder to learn ... . For suppose that you should think that a man had had a long voyage who had been caught in a raging storm as he left harbour and carried hither and thither and driven round and round in a circle by opposing winds? He did not have a long voyage, just a long tossing about.'

It's so important to remember the essential truth: life consists of what we are thinking all day long. The whirling gusts of busyness, money, technology and opinion drive us side to side while the buffeting currents of inconsequential, slights, wants and fears swirl us in circles.

The German philosopher Martin Heidegger feared that technology might reach such a level that it would 'so captivate, bewitch, dazzle, and beguile man that calculative thinking may someday come to be ... the only way of thinking.'

We would become unable to reflect upon the things that mattered to us. The sort of things that, in their final days, people say they wish they had spent more time on find no space in such a world.

At least not until it's too late.

The Sargasso Sea of the mind leaves no time to work out what's important to you. Instead it tugs your attention by the sleeve and pulls your mind into narrow alleyways where you fret about the next task and the next task and the next beep. Your thoughts have no time to deepen; your ambitions become trivial unless you give your thoughts some space.

"Excellent Sheep"

Talking about the importance of working out what's important to YOU have you heard of the phrase, "Excellent Sheep" ? It's a metaphor that describes an awful lot of modern life.

The writer and critic William Deresiewicz recently warned that the modern education system was creating students who strived to be "excellent sheep".

Excellent Sheep, he says, are people who seek to keep scoring highly in the challenges that are put before them. But they do not stop (or have the time to stop) and reflect upon the achievements they are pursuing.

They may be working hard and sacrifice much of their life in order to win laurels and triumph – but ultimately they are in danger of succeeding in things that don't really matter to them.

In other words they are using their minds (unlike the sea squirt – chalk it up!) but they are not using it to achieve the things that have meaning to them (d'oh!).

People don't have time to reflect because they are always "on" – always connected, always pursuing the next objective, but rarely heading towards their true north.

They are deep in the Sargasso Sea of other peoples thoughts.

James Dean, died in the way legend needs some of its heroes to succumb; young and boldly. He was a talented racing driver as well as a screen idol and the end came when his speeding Porsche Spyder convertible crashed as he zoomed to get to a race in Salinas, California.

He was already one of the biggest stars in Hollywood at the tender age of 24.

He only made three films and each was a blockbuster: *East of Eden*, *Giant* and, most famously, *Rebel without a Cause*.

The man who wrote the screenplay for *Rebel without a Cause* – the classic film of teenage disillusionment and discontent – was Stewart Stern.

After the funeral he wrote to Dean's parents and reflected upon the tragic loss of their son, his friend. He found consolation in the life that Dean had embraced every moment of. He had lived fully in his few years and this was a lesson. He told them:

'From Jimmy I have learned the value of a minute. He loved his minutes and I shall now love mine.'

And the minute hand ticks by even as you read this.
Every day it circles the clock 1,440 times.
How many of those minutes will you value?

Every year it swings by another 500,000 times.
Each of them is yours. How many of them will you love?

Appreciate and contemplate

The skill of thinking big lies in the art of appreciation.

It demands that you work out what really matters to you.

Appreciating life while you are in the thick of it is the most indulgent thing you can do. It is highly recommended.

As Ferris Bueller said: 'Life moves pretty fast. If you don't stop and look around once in a while, you could miss it.'

We know it, yet we don't do it.

Despite being surrounded by productivity-enhancing and life-improving gadgets, tablets, robots, sensors, beeps and invisible data clouds somehow we're no less busy than we used to be.

As a result we rarely take time to simply be; to contemplate the wonders of life and the Universe.

This is a mistake. Contemplation of what really matters is one of life's great joys. Mistakenly we put off such thoughts until the day when we retire (an increasingly far off and unlikely occasion for most of us).

As Seneca warned a young friend, in days when people died much younger than we do:

> 'How late it is to begin really to live just when life must end. How stupid to forget our mortality and put off sensible plans to our fiftieth and sixtieth years, arriving to begin life from a point at which few have arrived!'

LIFE OUTSIDE THE VORTEX OF GARBAGE
PUT YOUR ENERGY THERE
WORK OUT WHAT REALLY MATTERS
LOVE YOUR MINUTES
THINKING BIG

Start enjoying the important things now and you may find that Massive Monday never comes round again. You may learn how to enjoy the world more. Or you may finally admit that what you pretend to enjoy today you really don't.

In this way, through the art of appreciation, you will work out what really matters to you.

I was struck by some plain-speaking advice from Nicholas Negroponte who was an adviser to Bill Clinton, founded the One Laptop per Child programme and co-founded the MIT Media Laboratory which is responsible for much of the amazing new Internet technology that changes our lives.

His view was that technology increases the chance that people can turn their avocation into a business. An avocation is traditionally the thing that you are passionate about but which is not how you earn a living. Bruce Wayne's vocation was as an industrialist/playboy. His avocation was crime fighting in a rubber suit. Woody Allen's vocation is a film director, his avocation is a jazz musician.

According to Negroponte:

> 'It's, in fact, a period today where you can take an avocation and turn it into something that's very intimately connected with what you do. And if you are toying with taking a job because it pays well but you hate it, don't do that.'

Maybe it's because life moves so fast that in more modern times, Seneca's sagacious advice to his young friend on not waiting til it's too late to appreciate life, was stripped down to a mere three words by David Foster Wallace.

He said that learning to think about things beyond the wants, hurts and frustrations of your unconscious mind is the only way to achieve 'life before death'.

Unless we make a conscious effort, Foster Wallace said, then we are no more aware of the wonders of life and the things that matter than a fish is aware of water.

Parkinson's law states that work expands to fill the available time. Since you are available all the time in this perma-connected world, work has expanded to fill every waking hour.

You could just switch off your devices when the work day is finished. Leave the Sargasso Sea at the office. Impossible you think?

Google recently ran a project in Dublin in which members of staff were asked to drop off anything that beeped at the front desk before they went home. Staff went home with no work phones, no work email, no tablet or laptop.

'Googlers' reported blissful, stressless evenings.

This sounds like a perfect emotional state to think big.

Think about it. Then try it. Maybe even switch your phone off from time to time. You might be less indispensable than your ego thinks.

You too may enjoy blissful, stressless evenings. And the world may yet continue to spin.

R. Buckminster Fuller had a wonderful name. He had an even more wonderful mind. He was a sort of philosopher-engineer and he felt that the correct way to think about the planet Earth was that it was a spaceship.

He worried that people were so occupied by their work that they had little time to contemplate the wonders of the Universe they were flying through on their spaceship.

His hope was that robots, computers and automation would free workers from their labour so that they would be able to ask themselves:

'What was it I was thinking that fascinated me so, before I was told I had to do something else in order to make a living.'

Important stuff can't be measured

The world has never been more measurable. Digitization lets us measure everything: weigh it, quantify it, evaluate it, predict it, crowd source ratings and boil it all down to a single number, to a thumbs up or a five star rating.

1. This has its uses. But it can't handle the complexity of human experience.
2. If the world is only swayed by things that are measurable then we should hear from an economist.
3. Economists deal with mathematics and want to know what can be measured.

Economists are so serious that at some universities they wear white lab coats to declare that they are 'real scientists' while other 'social scientists' – such as sociologists, anthropologists, historians, political scientists and philosophers and so on – are frivolous.

In 1934 the economist Dr Simon Kuznets was asked by the US Congress to devise a single number that could be reported regularly in order to give a status report on the entire economy. Kuznets invented a measure of national income called Gross Domestic Product (GDP).

His idea swept the world. GDP is now the measure used in almost every civil service, parliament and news programme in the world to evaluate and report on economic health.

And yet Kuznets regretted the singular importance that was attached to it. It has limitations.

He said:

> 'No income measurement undertakes to estimate the reverse side of income, that is, the intensity and unpleasantness of effort going into the earning of the income. The welfare of a nation can, therefore, scarcely be inferred from a measurement of national income as defined [by GDP].'

His point is that there is more to life than dollars and pounds and expensive shoes and watches.

Kuznets' message is obvious. But we find it hard to remember the obvious.

So let's be clear: life has more to offer than bling and the sweat that pays for it.

LIFE HAS MORE TO OFFER THAN BLING AND THE SWEAT THAT PAYS FOR IT

The influential twentieth-century philosopher Bertrand Russell once complained that 'the notion that the desirable activities are those that bring a profit has made everything topsy-turvy.'

Such topsy-turvy priorities drag our mind hither and thither. It's another thing that stops us working out what matters to us, and being able to consciously decide where we want to apply our ambition and energy.

The cult of busyness

The humble act of working out what's important to you already starts moving you towards it. This might be working to build your company, get a promotion, afford a holiday, write a book, evolve into a better artist or become more mindful.

Working to this end is being productive.

Working for the sake of work is not. Much teaching, conditioning and preaching has told us that working is a virtue in its own right. This is dubious.

This idea is the corner-stone of the cult of busyness. In order to maintain this notion, observed Russell, the rich 'preach the dignity of labour, while taking care to remain undignified in this respect.'

As someone else once pointed out, when it comes to work, 'It is only those who tell others what to do who laud its virtues'.

Maybe you are a member of the busyness cult. You probably are.

MEMBERS OF THE CULT OF BUSYNESS
ARE OFTEN FOUND IN THE MIRROR

Snakeskin

A snake sheds its skin. It lives some more. It travels and grows. And it sheds its skin again.

The skin it leaves behind is a unique product of the individual snake's life.

And it is beautiful.

Your ideas are the product of your life experience.

If you escape the clutter then you can release your imagination. You will create art, empathy, creativity, imagination, innovation, and human connection, and this will be a legacy of your journey like the skin shed by the snake as it grows bigger.

It takes courage, determination and practice to harness your ideas but the prize is worth it. Because they are as unique as your life is. Your ideas are the product of your unique view of the world informed by the bumps, twists and turns of your particular journey.

These are your white horses. Creative, new, interesting and precious.

And like the snakeskin you will produce more and bigger ideas as you grow.

'Businesses everywhere say they need people who are creative and think independently. But the argument is not just about businesses. It's about having lives with purpose and meaning in and beyond whatever work we do.'

Sir Ken Robinson

It's hard to love a fake

Nobody wants to hire you or hang out with you because you think like the next person. They did once, it is true. But those days are gone. Now what counts is that you have original ideas and bring yourself to the table.

The Indie band Death Cab for Cutie wore blue ribbons to the Grammys in 2009. 'We're here to raise awareness of Auto-Tuner abuse', they explained.

Auto-Tune is a technology that enables a producer to transform the pitch of a singer's off key, real life warble and magically turn it onto the intended vocal line. In other words it can make anybody – anybody – a competent pop singer.

The same technology can also correct the clumsy notes by the keyboard player, the wrong drum beat, slipshod accuracy by the lead guitarist and so on.

'A little use is OK, but there is a difference between "use" and "abuse", and I feel we're getting to a point of abuse at this point', a member of the band told MTV.

The problem, they added, is that 'musicians of tomorrow will never practice. They will never try to be good, because yeah, you can do it just on the computer.'

The first time I heard Auto-Tune was on the single 'Believe' by Cher in 1998. The Auto-Tune was cranked up to create a deliberately weird, robotic sci-fi sound. That was creative.

But since then the technology has swept through the industry and been used to transform pre-packaged singers and bands with the right 'look' into short-lived pop stars.

In pop it seems that almost everyone uses Auto-Tune but almost no-one admits to it.

And there's the rub. They daren't own up. The problem with admitting to it is that the audience suddenly feel duped. The singer is no longer bringing soul to the song; they're faking it.

And you can't fall in love with that.

In 2010 fans of the TV talent show *The X-Factor* protested when it was 'X-Posed' that producers were using Auto-Tune to make some singers sound better than they really were … and others worse.

'The implication is that these singers are not the authors of their own destiny; they are merely following a script penned by the show's creators that is set to end in a flurry of glitter cannons and another bloodless cover version at No 1 come December. It seems as though the show's producers are sneering at their own loyal viewers', wrote *The Guardian*.

So the music industry has an authentic voice problem. Literally.

It never used to be that way.

Neil Young, Bob Dylan and Leonard Cohen wouldn't have made it in a world of Auto-Tune. Or rather they'd make it but they'd sound like everyone else.

And this is the crux of the matter. It is precisely the flaws, the strain and the emotion in the expression of the song that makes us love singers and their voices. It's the unique pattern of their particular snakeskin. When they think big they don't seek to duplicate someone else. They seek to be them as you must seek to be you.

I recently read that John Lennon hated his voice and found it 'thin and reedy' – and learning this level of self-doubt and anxiety made me love his singing voice even more than I used to.

The same is true with thinking big and bringing your white horse to the shore. To expand your thinking and connect your ideas with the rest of the world you must escape the Sargasso Sea of the mind and bring yourself to the table.

People can't connect with fake. They don't value it because it's not special.

As Seth Godin wrote, 'People pay more for the unexpected, the scarce and the valuable.'

They fall in love with the authentic.

'Nothing comes from Nothing.'

King Lear, Shakespeare

'You will find only what you bring in.'

Yoda

'The unfed mind devours itself.'

Gore Vidal

FEED YOUR MIND

The cargo cults

In the South Pacific islands of New Guinea and Vanuatu some people don't know any better.

Here, lie some islands and tribes which are almost untouched by the modern world.

Alas, they have been touched. A little bit. Just enough to cause trouble.

And now they practice the cult of cargo planes.

HERE BE CARGO CULTS

You see, during World War 2 the islands were stop off points for military cargo aircraft.

And the islanders could not fail to notice that these strange looking people who had suddenly appeared on their land were blessed with food, elaborate clothes and all manner of machinery and other gifts.

Weirdest of all, these strangers never hunted for food, nor did they grow it. They never made anything, nor did they ever repair anything. Yet they had everything.

How could this be? They observed their behaviour.

Instead of doing anything productive they engaged in strange rituals – for example, they wore identical clothes and marched in formation to no particular place and back again, they listened to voices from boxes, they saluted each other, they built runways and control towers, and then they sat at tables all day and made marks on paper.

But oh boy, did this please the Gods. They loved these rituals!

Because lo! from the heavens descended giant mechanical birds full of gifts.

As the islanders knew nothing of factories, supply chains, production lines or lean manufacturing processes they assumed that these goods appeared fully formed, summoned as gifts from deities, responding to the peculiar rituals of the strangers.

So after the war, when the planes had left, they cultishly mimicked the weird strangers. The rituals of the cargo cult involve building replica runways, control towers from sticks, headphones from straw, wooden boxes and synchronized marching.

...But of course nothing ever comes.

ON THE SUBJECT OF WAITING FOR SOMETHING THAT NEVER COMES

The problem with cargo cults is not a lack of imagination.

They have an explanation for what is happening that is perfectly reasonable given what they know of the world. In their particular pidgin they gasped:

'OMG! Our ancestors in heaven have been tricked to send gifts to the weird but scheming strangers.'

No, the problem is not a lack of imagination. The problem is not knowing enough.

And this is another lesson for thinking big.

It's not sufficient to be interested in principle. You must be interested in practice.

If you have a passion for something, an ambition to be somewhere, an appetite to change direction then you must immerse yourself in that thing. Nothing of consequence has ever been achieved without someone first throwing themselves passionately into the field.

It's not just stone-age tribes. Highly intelligent species from outer space can also fail to do enough research. Ford Prefect is an

YOU CAN'T SKIM YOUR WAY to GREATNESS

inter-galactic hitchhiker in Douglas Adam's book, radio show, play and film *The Hitchhiker's Guide To The Galaxy*.

Ford's real name is, according to Adams, 'only pronounceable in an obscure Betelgeusian dialect'.

So when he comes to the planet Earth he takes on a fake Earth name in order to blend in with the Earthian inhabitants. But he only did the briefest research and chooses the name Ford Prefect since this appears to him to be the name of 'the dominant life form' on the planet.

The Ford Prefect was, in fact, a British car manufactured from 1938 to 1961.

To repeat: the lesson from primitive cargo cults and advanced

interstellar travellers is this: the more you know about the things that fascinate you the better your thinking will be.

The truth is in and it's clear. The more you immerse yourself in the world, the more you will marvel at it and the more of its problems you will solve.

Whatever you are actively and passionately interested in the more you will know about it, and the more you know the more creative you can be. Even your errors will be better.

Bathe your mind in the rich stew of human knowledge

Here's the nub of it. The more you steal, filch and pilfer knowledge and inspiration from others the more shoulders you can stand on.

The secret to making your ideas really big is to bathe your mind in the rich stew of human knowledge and, now that you have found yourself, take special care to pay attention to the things that you are most passionate about.

As Hart Crane, said of words, which were his passion as you'd expect of a famous poet: 'One must be drenched in words, literally soaked in them, to have the right ones form themselves into the proper patterns at the right moment.'

This is a magic stew. The more people take from it, the more they contribute to it by subsequently thinking bigger.

You are a mashup of what you let into your life, said the writer Austin Kleon.

Bird watching and this year's hot colour

You cannot be interesting if you are not interested.

Being interested, investing yourself in some aspect of the world, makes things happen and starts chain reactions of other interesting things.

The most nerdy of interests can lead to the most unexpected developments.

A hundred years ago Robert Ridgway, chief bird watcher of the famous Smithsonian museum, needed a better way to differentiate bird species. Obviously he focused on their feathers.

His interest in feathers led him to be interested in colours. He immersed himself in the study of colours and by 1912 he had identified, labelled and indexed 1,115 colours, which he collected in a self-published book called *Color Standards and Color Nomenclature*.

Dragon's Blood Red and Light Paris Green were just two of the colours he described. This gives an idea of how much imagination and interest he brought to the subject.

There were other books but his was the most comprehensive. Daniel Lewis, the author of *The Feathery Tribe: Robert Ridgway and the Modern Study of Birds*, wrote that in 1905 the French Society of Chrysanthemists, created a two-volume set of swatches and names for their own botanical uses. 'Holly Green' was described as 'the ordinary color of the foliage of the common holly, viewed from 1 to 2 meters away, and without considering reflections.' And despite the fact that the work was meant for international consumption, its soul remained French. 'Sky Blue', for example, was described as 'The color reminiscent of pure sky, in summer (in the climate of Paris).'

The study of colours turned out to be valuable far beyond the world of ornithology.

Ridgway's book became the model for the Pantone business which today, 100 years later, is ready to tell you that the hot colour of 2014 is 'Radiant Orchid'. The company which was bought for $180m in 2007 declares every 12 months what is the colour of the year. Radiant Orchid is a shade of purple that emanates 'confidence in your creativity'.

You'll see Radiant Orchid on trainers, the trim on cool clothing and accessories and on stationary.

Knowing about colours is big business. The company that pronounces the colour of the year has produced colour charts that are used by designers all over the world. Pantone colour books enable a consistency in colours. This ensures a designer in Shanghai knows what a designer in Berlin means when they say Dragon's Blood Red.

The colour of 2013 was Emerald. In case you'd forgotten.

The original ideas that you have, the idle thoughts and the sudden rush of insights that fall upon you as if from thin air, in truth come from everything that you have already let into your mind.

The more shoulders you can climb on the higher you can reach.

If you let in greatness then you cannot help but let greatness influence your thoughts and in turn, your life.

If nothing is entirely original and everything is built on what has come before then commit to knowing as much as possible of what has come before. The more shoulders you can climb on the higher you can reach.

Draw deeply from the stew of human knowledge and your thinking will grow in richness and scope. Like, the great view from the top of a tower, it comes from having climbed all the steps.

This is not a recipe for mere duplication.

Good artists copy, great artists steal, said Picasso.

'He who resolves never to ransack any mind but his own ... will be obliged to imitate himself', said Joshua Reynolds.

When you take what someone else has created and you bring it into your life you see the world anew and what you create is the stolen idea reflected in the glassy wave of your personal journey.

This is true whether you are growing your ambition, your art, your business or any aspect of your life.

ON THE MENU

KNOWLEDGE
PASSION
HEROES
MENTORS
IDLENESS
COMPETITORS
SOLITUDE
DEBATE + DISSENT
CONTEMPLATION

You are not a tabula rasa

This is a term used by philosophers who like to debate whether the mind of a new born baby is a clean slate – tabula rasa – that only becomes a unique personality over time or whether some genetically pre-coded behaviours and biases are already baked in.

For our purposes this doesn't matter. If you're reading this then you ain't no tabula rasa.

You are the sum of all that you have experienced – good and bad.

Whatever is in this bag of experience and knowledge is the raw material from which your ideas will grow. And if knowledge is missing – go get it.

Mash it up

Big ideas, insights, ambition and new perspectives are the product of the collision of ideas.

It's the combination of ideas in a novel way that produces the next new idea.

It's a mashup process.

A DJ can only mix the music she knows. Her breadth of music knowledge defines the parameter of her range.

The more you know, the more you can choose from. The more opportunity you have to bring something unique into the world.

You might be applying knowledge from one area to another such as statistical analysis from finance to baseball as in the story made famous by Moneyball. Or you might be applying your knowledge of winepresses to your expertise as a goldsmith as Gutenberg did when he partnered with the owner of a paper mill to invent the printing press.

Auto-Tune was the creation of a geologist who went back to school and added music composition to his mashup bag of skills and interest. He realized he could use the science of manipulating frequencies – as seismologists do – in the music industry.

Or you might take the ideas that Carl Jung the psychoanalyst had about the human psyche and cultural archetypes and develop from that an anthropological model of human story telling that unites all the stories of the world as Joseph Campbell did.

And you might say wow! that resonates with me – it twangs! – and use it as the model for your blockbuster film as George Lucas did when he wrote Star Wars.

But you need to know this stuff in the first place.

And that means you have to take a passionate interest in the world.

JOSEPH CAMPBELL

...defined the "monomyth" common to all legends of all cultures and times:

"A hero ventures forth from the world of common day into a region of supernatural wonder: fabulous forces are there encountered and a decisive victory is won: the hero comes back from this mysterious adventure with the power to bestow boons on his fellow man."

STAR WARS

...is the "monomyth" interpreted as a space-western by George Lucas:

Plucked from a peaceful homestead on Tatooine, Luke Skywalker is plunged into a new world of aliens, rebels and the Empire's henchmen. He must confront Darth Vader, become a Jedi Knight and destroy the Death Star to liberate the Galaxy.

Hotei's mashup bag

Hotei is the well-rounded, laughing monk you have seen in statues, figurines and paintings.

This is the thing:

Hotei had a bag. You'll see it in his hand or slung over his shoulder in every image of him.

In this bag existed everything.

He could help people out of all sorts of predicaments by fishing around in his bag for what was needed.

The more he had in there the more problems he could solve. And he had everything.

You want a mind like Hotei's bag. Fill it with wonderful things that fire up your passion and excite your mind. Think of it like a mental mashup bag. The more that you have inside the bigger your ambition, the more informed your thinking, the more colourful the spectrum of your inspiration.

Bring a long, broad spoon

The secret to inspiration and serendipity is to reach *deep* into the areas that fascinate and enliven you and wake you up in the morning while, at the same time, stretching *across*, gathering as much general knowledge about the universe as you can, and in so doing, broaden the distant corners of your experience.

As well as reaching into the far corners of the stew where the surprising things are, you want to go deep into the areas that you are really passionate about.

This is the stuff that excites you the most. You might have learned what this is by creating space in the Sargasso Sea of the mind and bringing yourself to the table. This is how you have decided to use your brain.

Benjamin Hoff wrote the best-selling book *The Tao of Pooh* in the evenings and at weekends while he was working as a tree pruner in a Japanese garden in Portland, Oregon.

I thought that was interesting and checked his website. It turns out that he can't stop dipping into the stew of knowledge. His biography notes that he 'has been a writer, an investigative photojournalist, a tree pruner, a songwriter, and a recording musician and singer. He has studied architecture, music, fine arts, graphic design, and Asian culture – including Japanese Tea Ceremony (third certificate level), Japanese fine-pruning methods (two years of apprenticeship), and the comparatively esoteric martial-art form of T'ai Chi Ch'uan (four years of instruction, including a year of Ch'i Kung)'.

The sci-fi writer Isaac Asimov was once asked whether he thought that we could learn, at any time of life, anything that strikes our fancy.

He replied: 'The key words here are "that strikes our fancy". There are some things that simply don't strike my fancy, and I doubt that I can force myself to be educated in them. On the other hand when there's a subject I'm ferociously interested in, then it's easy for me to learn about it. I take it in gradually and cheerfully'.

Thanks to the Internet, this wealth of knowledge is so easy to access, so instant that we mistakenly forget how suddenly and how recently this new and wonderful boon arrived. It's not just the children of the Internet age who don't know any different. We're in danger of forgetting it ourselves.

Buckminster Fuller talked about the 'ease and speed with which the transformed reality becomes so "natural" as mis-seemingly to have always been obvious.'

So please: don't take it for granted. Use it!

Tyler Cowen, the academic and best-selling author said: 'The more information that's out there, the greater the returns to just being willing to sit down and apply yourself. Information isn't what's scarce; it's the willingness to do something with it.'

A broad interest in life will allow the serendipitous mashup to happen, it will open your horizons, deepen your dreams and expand your ambition.

The solution – whether it is the plot of a novel, a new method of manufacturing or working out your switch in career – is very often the product of transferring knowhow from elsewhere to your current situation. This is what makes the impossible a very rare thing indeed. There is nearly always a way. But you need to let your mind out into the Universe to find it.

 ## A practical tip – stop for 30 seconds

To get the most from splashing around in great ideas, inspiration and new experiences you ought to take a moment.

It is simple but takes a little discipline. Start practising this right now. Take 30 seconds to reflect on what you have learned. Do this after each interaction with someone, with an idea, with some art, with nature, with an insight.

This act of thinking about what was good will reinforce the remembrance of it. Reflection at the end of the day, or the end of a lecture, a TED video, an article you read, a visit to your therapist or an afternoon surfing will secure more value from that experience.

The scientist Giada di Stefano described it as 'the intentional attempt to synthesize, abstract and articulate the key lessons taught by experience.'

Sportsmen, salesmen and business executives are shown to learn better from experience and achieve higher future performance just so long as they simply take a moment to stop and deliberately think about the thing they just experienced.

When you stop the world for a moment your mind recognizes that this must be important. This places the experience in a more accessible place in your mind. It's how your mind decides what, from everything you experience, you will intentionally carry with you and place near the top of your mashup bag.

Throw some people in your mashup bag

Surround yourself not just with ideas but also with the people who bring out good ideas, who inspire, lead and encourage you to go further.

Most of all surround yourself with people that inspire you to enjoy your life. That way you'll go further whatever happens. When you're having fun at anything then you have increased powers of persistence. You don't need a scientist to tell you this: your life experience will.

But here's a scientist telling you anyway! Daniel Kahneman won a Nobel Prize for his work in economics and also wrote the best-selling book Thinking Fast and Slow.

He recounts in his biography the transformatory experience of working with a colleague, Amos Tversky:

'The experience was magical. I had enjoyed collaborative work before, but this was something different. Amos was often described by people who knew him as the smartest person they knew. He was also very funny, with an endless supply of jokes appropriate to every nuance of a situation. In his presence, I became funny as well, and the result was that we could spend hours of solid work in continuous mirth ... I have probably shared more than half of the laughs of my life with Amos.'

As you free your mind to think big and release your white horses, surround yourself, like Kahneman did, with people that make you a better person.

i. Have heroes

If it's art then study the artists you admire; whatever your field, study the leading lights – find out everything you can about the people who lead great teams; who innovate; who design; cook; dance; sing; pot; write, sculpt; sail; travel.

Read obituaries to understand how people you respect lived their lives and what obstacles they overcame and how.

You will be surprised how much heroes can spur you to go one step further. Hemingway, when he received his Nobel Prize, explained how it was the great work of previous writers that forced new writers to stretch themselves and go further with their thoughts and ambition. He competed with his heroes!

Psychologists have shown that simply having heroes who have also overcome hardships or travelled the same path as you will help you triumph.

In one study, children from bad neighbourhoods who had thrived despite poor schools and generally low life chances were found to have done so and defied the odds because they learned about famous people who had overcome similar obstacles.

The knowledge that determination, hard work and self-belief had enabled others to prevail against challenges increased the chances that they would do the same.

In other words they could mashup the realities of their environment with the possibilities revealed by others and so light up the path to an alternative reality for themselves.

ii. Seek different opinions

Among the many thinking disciplines of Charlie Munger, one of the world's most successful investors, he insists on reading the opinions of people he disagrees with. It's how he keeps challenging his own thoughts and opinions and prevents them going stale.

If you only read and listen to people who agree with you then you're likely to just entrench your thinking and learn nothing new.

iii. Play with a high quality band

Whether you're playing tennis, jamming in a band, writing code, doing yoga or singing karaoke the quality of what you do will be brought up by the standards around you.

This is why you should visit art galleries, read great authors, visit gardens or do whatever you can to expose yourself to inspiration.

...And be warned: the reverse is also true.

The special ingredient – idleness!

There is a magical and surprising ingredient to thinking big. It is idleness.

Idleness is craved by the mind but we find it hard to feed the mind with idleness because it doesn't seem to be a productive thing. After all you live amidst the cult of busyness. If you're reading this book it's because you want to DO things. So idleness feels like a crazy thing to be packing into your mashup bag.

But you must. Don't think of it as laziness. Idleness is the magic catalyst that creates the alchemy of thinking big from all the inspiration, knowledge and deep thought you're feeding on.

Throughout the ages great minds have taught that it is more than just knowledge and ideas that you need to feed your mind.

You need to give it time and space and this is probably the hardest thing of all. It's how you stay out of the Sargasso Sea of the mind and think bigger.

In the age of perma-connected busyness there are two forms of idleness which deserve special attention:

- disciplined stillness through meditation
- the pursuit of idle knowledge.

Idleness type 1 – stillness

The psychologist and writer Ed Hallowell described the way many of us feel:

> 'Having treated Attention Deficit Disorder since 1981, I began to see an upsurge in the mid 1990s in the number of people who complained of being chronically inattentive, disorganised and overbooked. Many came to me wondering if they had ADD. While some did, most did not. Instead they had what I called a severe case of modern life.'

The solution for peace of mind and for fresh and creative problem solving and thinking big is creating room in our lives for a state of idleness and learning to switch off the hubbub of noise swirling around our heads through learning meditation.

The billionaire head of the world's largest hedge fund, Ray Dalio of Bridgewater Associates said:

> 'Meditation, more than any other factor, has been the reason for what success I've had. If there's stress, I'll just break off and go into the meditation. It will just wash off of me.'

Josh Zwaitken, who became the US chess champion at the age of 16 and a champion martial artist at the age of 20, coaches high performance to leading sportsmen and business people. He says meditation is critical to allow you to achieve 'presence' which lets you get through the mental swirl.

Zwaitken trains elite performers to achieve better results at whatever it is they do – from sports to financial trading. He encourages them to meditate to find the head space to find their core essence – their authentic voice.

He told the author Tim Ferris how important it is to understand how you think and approach using your mind in any field. Naturally he speaks about chess:

> 'To be world class you need to express the core of your being through your art – I think this is true of many arts – you can have a very mathematical person who plays chess very mathematically, you can have a very musical person who plays chess musically. Someone might be much more kinesthetic like myself and sort of a feeling for flow and hidden harmonies and almost a physically energetic relationship to chess.'

Idleness type 2 – idle knowledge

The cult of busyness requires a certain type of thinking. You could call it instrumental thinking. The consequences of the thinking must be instrumental in achieving value: sales, innovation, cost savings... wealth and power.

This is valuable but it is narrow, focused and constrained.

Idle thinking is the opposite of this. Idle thinking finds the value of knowledge in itself. Of course the cult of busyness would see this as just so much loafing around.

And yet idle thinking, knowledge for the sake of knowledge rather than the money or power it might bring you, is one of life's great joys.

Bertrand Russell explained how knowledge of the history of the apricot makes the experience of eating one more pleasurable even though it doesn't actually materially change anything.

Make up your own mind.

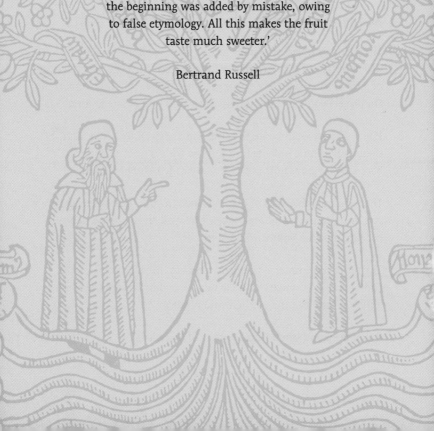

'Curious learning not only makes unpleasant things less unpleasant, but also makes pleasant things more pleasant. I have enjoyed peaches and apricots more since I have known that they were first cultivated in China in the early days of the Han dynasty; that Chinese hostages held by the great King Kaniska introduced them into India, whence they spread to Persia, reaching the Roman Empire in the first Century of our era; that the word "apricot" is derived from the same Latin source as the word "precocious", because the apricot ripens early; and that the A at the beginning was added by mistake, owing to false etymology. All this makes the fruit taste much sweeter.'

Bertrand Russell

And one more sprinkle of idleness magic

Allowing idleness into your life will not just make you more creative, allow you to foster more ideas, understand your own priorities and enjoy the moment. It's quite simply healthier.

In his book, Autopilot; The Art and Science of Doing Nothing, Andrew Smart wrote: 'Neuroscientific evidence argues that your brain needs to rest, right now. While our minds are exquisitely evolved for intense action, in order to function normally our brains also need to be idle – a lot of the time it turns out.'

He adds: 'In the short term busyness destroys creativity, self-knowledge, emotional well-being, your ability to be social – and it can damage your cardiovascular health.'

A final thought about the cargo cults

The islanders operated a so-called 'Big Man' political system in which influence was rewarded and reinforced through the exchange of gifts. In such a society, the more you can give the more important (or bigger) you are... and the harder it is to reciprocate in kind.

If you cannot reciprocate the gifts you are given by a 'Big Man' then you become indebted. And those who cannot reciprocate because they have nothing to give are called 'Rubbish Men'.

The most valuable gifts of all are rooted in your ideas. The gifts you bring to the world are those which you create and which you conjure up from your thinking big.

The more you immerse yourself in heroes, in ideas, in contemplative thought, in a passionate and interested life the more gifts you have to offer in the world of ideas.

Reach deep and often into the stew of knowledge.

tHE HEDgEHog AND tHE FoX

The fox has many strategies to escape its pursuers.

It can outrun them, it can hide in burrows, it can double-back on its tracks to lay a false scent trail. It can climb trees, roll in muck to mask its scent, swim in rivers and it can even talk itself out of trouble.

The hedgehog has but a single strategy. It cannot run fast. It is not a smooth talker. It knows what it will do: roll into a spiky ball and stay like that. Prickly and inedible. It persists.

The fox can do many things pretty well. The hedgehog does one thing very well indeed.

As an ancient Greek proverb states: *"The fox knows many things, but the hedgehog knows one big thing."*

The philosopher Isiah Berlin famously used the story to categorise thinkers into two types. Hedgehog thinkers have a single, unifying view of the world through which they fit every new piece of information or argument they come across. Let us say they are specialists.

The fox adapts their way of thinking to the circumstances facing them. You could call them a jack of all (thinking) trades. Or free thinkers – which sounds less critical.

Neither approach is in principal right or wrong. Most of the time your best advice will be to negotiate a balance between the two. A hedgehog-like focus on one thing will increase your chances of success in that thing; a fox-like broad knowledge will give you the most options.

'He could "discover the splendours of the world like cigarette butts in ashtrays".'

Franz Kafka said of the wit Peter Altenberg

'Discovery consists of seeing what everybody has seen and thinking what nobody has thought.'

Albert Sent-Gyorgyi

Habit 4

Notice Things

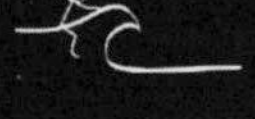

Oh…

Head up, lights on, ears pricked, throw down the drawbridge, cross the moat of the closed mind and learn to recognize that feeling when something amazing and inspirational is happening right before your very eyes.

You'll know it when it happens. Just so long as you know what to look for.

And what you need to look for is the feeling that something curious just happened and merits 30 seconds of contemplation.

The physicist and sci-fi writer Isaac Asimov explained that the most exciting phrase to hear in science, the one that heralds new discoveries, is not 'Eureka!' (I found it!) but rather, 'hmm... that's funny...'.

Wobbliness and a razor sharp mind

The Universe is ceaselessly trying to show us things. All we have to do is notice. But noticing is hard. Or rather, not noticing is easy.

The mind needs to be alert and yet idle and open at the same time.

This was the state of mind of Richard Feynman when he noticed something that led to a Nobel Prize for physics. Years later, Feynman said the moment of registering what he had noticed was like a cork coming out of a bottle: 'Everything just poured out.'

'That afternoon while I was eating lunch, some kid threw up a plate in the cafeteria', he explained. 'There was a blue medallion on the plate, the Cornell sign, and as he threw up the plate and it came down, the blue thing went around and it seemed to me that the blue thing went round faster than the wobble, and I wondered what the relationship was between the two.

'I was just playing, no importance at all, but I played around with the equations of motion of rotating things, and I found out that if the wobble is small the blue thing goes around twice as fast as the wobble goes round.'

He doodled some thoughts on a napkin and carried on with his day. Sensing that there was something important in what he had noticed Feynman came back to his equations and worked away at the relationship. This was when he discovered that there was a two-to-one ratio in the relationship of wobble and spin.

In other words, when the plate was spinning slowly the plate wobbled at a rate exactly half of the rotation.

He showed his colleague, Hans Bethe, what he had discovered.

'But what's the importance of that?', Bethe asked.

'It doesn't have any importance', he said. 'I don't care whether a thing has importance. Isn't it fun?'

'It's fun', Bethe agreed.

Feynman told him that was all he was going to do from now on – 'have fun'.*

A bit like Bertrand Russell's history of the apricot, Feynman's wobbly plate is an instance of someone simply enjoying the contemplation and discovery of being part of the Universe.

And although it was fun, it reminded him of a problem about electron spin, described by Paul Dirac, another physicist, and this in turn led him back to Quantum Electrodynamics and this understanding of

---

* James Gleick, Genius: *The Life and Science of Richard Feynman*

spinning objects amounted in the end to a Nobel Prize. (That's as much as I will ever say about Quantum science and it's already a stretch.)

Lesson: heads up!

Hidden in plain sight

In fact, the Universe is waving flags, blowing raspberries, doing the can-can and fish-hooking you with inspiration, ideas and solutions. The sort of stuff that might make you scratch you head and say... 'that's funny'.

Noticing these moments and then plucking them is a skill. It demands of you only that you practice keeping your mind open and register the things that push your intuition buzzer.

The poet Robert Frost said that a poem 'begins as a lump in the throat, a sense of wrong, a homesickness, a lovesickness. It is never a thought to begin with.'

Your best idea, your most valuable insight about life or, say, where you want to go with your business may start out as a fragile wisp of an idea, like a dandelion seed floating past you on the merest puff of wind.

Sometimes a flicker of understanding fizzes by and we feel tantalizingly close to seeing the world a little more clearly. But then it evaporates almost as soon as we shift our mental gaze.

Other times the train of thought that may solve a puzzle can suddenly become heavy; immovable without another shove of the mind which is all of a sudden enmired in heavy cotton mud, unused to the effort of thinking.

These moments are your white horses.

THE UNIVERSE IS ALWAYS trying to SHOW YOU tHiNgs...

SPEED LIMIT 35

SPECIAL EVENT AHEAD

SoMETiMES it's JuST ROADWORKS

Many fortunes have been made by people who have applied the power of noticing. Other times the value comes in the form of a silent chuckle and that's a sufficient reward.

People notice faces the most.

An image of Mars taken by Viking Orbiter 1 appears to show a giant face on the surface of the planet. Some people believed that extra-terrestrials had colonized Mars and left this face as an enigmatic sign, like a whopping great graffiti tag: 'ET was here OK!'

Other faces have been revealed hidden in more accessible surfaces such as slices of toast, leaky walls, sticky buns and vegetables. The reason this happens is because the creator of the Universe wishes to communicate with mankind in a deliberately mysterious manner via baking, damp mould and groceries.

Think big and you will have your own opinion of this.

:-) (as they say on Mars)

The consolation of staring at your feet

I'VE HAD SO MANY PARKING TICKETS THAT I SEE YELLOW LINES IN MY SLEEP.

IT'S NO SURPRISE TO SEE THEM GRINNING IN REAL LIFE.

UNBURDENED BY
THE NARROW THINKING
OF ADULTHOOD,
MY NIECE WOULDN'T
LET ME FINISH THIS
PEAR.

I SAID : IT'S JUICY

SHE EXPLAINED: IT'S HAPPY

In any event, we are social animals and we are designed by many generations of evolution to spot and interpret faces. So noticing patterns that resemble faces is no big deal.

Noticing things other than faces demands more effort. Noticing ideas and solutions to problems is much harder, more valuable and is a skill worth honing.

A GOOD BAD SMELL

During World War 1 the mangled soldiers from the front were brought to Reading Hospital in Berkshire to be saved. It would take some four or five days for patients to arrive.

Given what medicine today knows about the 'Golden Hour', which is how important it is to treat someone correctly in the first hour of being injured, you can only begin to imagine the terrible life-chances of these soldiers.

Surgeon, Leonard Joyce noticed that the wounds that healed the fastest had a particular smell. He identified that the smell was caused by a particular bacteria, which became known as the Reading Bacillus. After experimenting with injured animals he took the bold step of applying bacteria to the wounds of humans.

Bear in mind that this was decades before the discovery of antibiotics. But it foretold the life-saving knowledge that there was such a thing as good bacteria. The Reading Bacillus cleaned the wound and did heal patients faster.

The lives saved by the Reading Bacillus were the result of the powers of noticing rather than any scientific insight about bacteria.

Practising noticing is nearly as hard as Practising letting butterflies land on your hand. You can't do it to command. The ideas will come when they want to, just like butterflies. But you have a much better chance if you wander out into the world. At least mentally.

If you spend your life literally or figuratively staring at your shoes when you walk instead of looking around then you're going to notice your shoe laces and the pavement but not much else. Not the film star who walked past you, the butterflies in the sky, or the person giving away free ice creams.

Head down, closed to the world and focused only inwardly you will miss the obvious and take the world for granted. The comedian Louis CK observed that when he was flying across the world on a jet plane a fellow passenger once got exasperated with the poor Wi-Fi connection.

'...But you're sitting in an armchair in the sky!' he exclaimed.

The same closed attitude will creep up on you when you invest the energy of your entire being into the small flat screen in the palm of your hand.

You won't notice, for example, the little moments of friction or surprise or confusion that might lead to something else; the spinning plate, the smell, the aching arms of the customers in your shop.

You might be aware of these things. But noticing it means consciously registering it. That's where the magic lies. That's thinking big.

Bringing it to the surface

'That's funny...' you say to yourself when your white horse bubbles up on the horizon.

Now stop everything! Let your mind dwell on what's funny. What are the implications? How can you apply this to your life, your business or your art?

How can you ride the white horse back to the shore?

Turn off the noise

The answer is you have to get away from the Sargasso Sea of the mind. To be able to notice things you must be able to step outside the state of pre-occupation.

> Boredom surfaces ideas like a grow bag produces tomatoes.

It is rare that we allow ourselves to simply observe the world. It's all too easy to reach for a device to occupy our minds, to plug music into our ears and drown out our subconscious, to invite social media noise into our heads, or catapult angry birds at forts and switch off our brains altogether.

Noticing, contemplation, inspiration, the next big thing often arises out of boredom; an unsung champion of thinking big. Smartphones have sucked the juice out of boredom. What used to be a rich and fertile compost for idle noticing, and contemplation is now desiccated. Like grains of sand boredom has been blown away by the distractions of silicon circuitry.

Reclaim it! Boredom surfaces ideas like a grow bag produces tomatoes.

People research this stuff. You'd be surprised. Several studies have demonstrated that creating a state of boredom through such tasks as reading a phone book prime the mind to think beyond the predefined rail road of normal, small thinking. Having been subjected to enforced boredom people are shown to be more creative subsequently.

Now, reading a phone book is never going to catch on and I know of no great artist or scientist who recommends it but accepting a state of boredom (or the fear of it) for 30 seconds before your mind takes off on a trip – that's definitely recommended.

And this is the good news; the restoration of the creative compost is easy. Switch it off, just sometimes. Open your ears, your eyes and your mind.

Be like a Rock God

Musicians are expert noticers.

Openness is the basis of jamming. All the members of a band notice what the others are doing and adapt to unexpected notes or chord changes. They adjust and make something creative out of it. Listening creates opportunities.

A musician friend once explained that the reason the live performances of so many rock songs end with an endless crescendo of crashing drums and thrashing guitars is that the band are all listening and looking at each other as they desperately try to synchronize the end of the song.

Write it down

Don't let these ideas escape. These precious wisps of inspiration that land on your hand will flutter away unless you decide to capture them right then.

Make a note. Write it on the palm of your hand. Type it onto your phone. Speak it into your voicemail.

Remember Richard Feynman – who idly noticed something interesting about the wobbly plate. He wrote down what he saw and his thoughts about it on a napkin. These were the notes he came back to. If it works for a bongo-playing Nobel Prize-winning physicist it might be worth copying that habit.

Because one thing I promise you: these starbursts of inspiration will be shifted aside by the next beep on your phone or toot from a taxi. You'll think 'no – this is brilliant I'll remember it'.

But the next thought will enter your mind like the nursery rhyme:

'And the little one said roll over, roll over. And they all rolled over and one fell out...'

Your short-term memory is already sweating because the cult of busyness demands it recalls a hundred things at once. And so, just as the dreams you have (which you're utterly convinced were so profound you'll never forget) soon evaporate – so your visiting inspiration will vanish.

The dandelion seed will float on past and the Universe will wave its flag, toot its horn, pull down its pants and moon at the next person.

Which is why, so often when you see some art, hear a story or read of a business triumph you say to yourself: 'But, I already thought of that.'

Write it down.

As you start deliberately making the effort to notice more you will have more to lose. The Universe and serendipity will appear to be visiting you more often. What's really happening is your eyes are open and your head is up. Open up your mashup bag and let it in. And when it does, commit here and now to making a note. It's so simple and the importance of it cannot be over-stated (no matter how much I try).

Write it down.

> 'As imagination bodies forth
> The forms of things unknown,
> the poet's pen
> Turns them to shapes and
> gives to airy nothing
> A local habitation and a name.'

Shakespeare, A Midsummer Night's Dream

Jootsing

Jumping Out Of The System, or "jootsing" is a phrase coined by the scientist Douglas Hofstadter.

When it hits you that there is a different way of achieving your goals, or living your life, by completely changing the way you think about your situation, then you are jootsing.

Jootsing is a branch of noticing.

To escape the rut, to leap ahead, to change the game or to swivel-and-pivot the first thing you must do is realize where you are. You must be *aware* of the rut.

In other words: To jump out of the system you must first notice that there is a system and you are in it.

As the US talk show host Dick Cavett quipped:

> "Howya gonna keep 'em down on the farm,
> after they've seen the farm?"

And these ruts are easily slipped into. We don't realize what has become our automatic thinking.

The philosopher Daniel Dennett explained how easily we slip into such traps: "Sometimes a problem gets started when somebody way-back-when said, '*Suppose for the sake of argument, that...*'" and folks agreed, for the sake of argument, and then in the subsequent parry and thrust everybody forgot how the problem started!"

To begin jootsing you need to switch off your automatic thinking. Then take a step back and notice the system, the unchallenged argument or your gilded cage.

'Then she lay on her back and gazed at the cloudless sky. Mr Beebe, whose opinion of her rose daily, whispered to his niece that that was the proper way to behave if any little thing went wrong.'

E.M. Forster, *A Room with a View*

'Embrace the suck.'

US Marine Corps

'Life is bristling with thorns, and I know no other remedy than to cultivate one's garden.'

Voltaire

CHANGE REALITY

(... Don't DENY it)

te the Hitchiker's Guide to the Galaxy,
rules govern how people react to

n the world when you're born is normal and
ord   t a natural part of the way the world works.

2. Anything that is invented between when you're 15 and 35 years old is new and exciting and revolutionary and you can probably get a career in it.

3. Anything invented after you're 35 is against the natural order of things.

> You can channel your energy into resisting change or making change. Not both.

This spirit of resistance is normal.

But it won't get you very far.

You can channel your energy into resisting change or making change. Not both.

Change is a constant and unavoidable part of our lives.

Technology is transforming our unstable reality at a mad gallop. Industries rise and fall, companies bubble up and burst (or get bought and assimilated), retailers know more about you than you do, advertisers stalk you around the Internet, people wear computers on their spectacles, and cars have no need for drivers.

Resistance, as the Daleks repeatedly and wearily explain to Dr Who, is useless.

But it doesn't stop us resisting change.

For some people resistance to change arises because the status quo is just tickety-boo-thank-you-very-much. These people tend to be fat cats, bosses, landlords, celebrities, sports stars and, in general, those who by luck or by luck-and-pluck are at the top of their tree.

But all of us, even those who should be clamouring for change of one sort or another, obey an instinct to fear change.

The unknown is scary.

And yet today, change is coming at you all day long. And when so much is possible you should be thinking bigger than ever.

If the known situation – the one you're living and experiencing today – is one that you want to change, or it's one that external forces are going to change anyway (redundancy, life change, relationship change, for example), then there is enormous benefit in not resisting it but accepting it and in this way becoming the architect of change from that place.

Accepting the reality of new technology's exhausting and exciting offspring – perpetual change – allows you to embrace progress and invest your mental energy building your ambition on top of the world as it is becoming, rather than the one you wished it still was. ...And may never have been.

Push and pull

Accept or resist is a decision you must make each time life throws something at you.

Resistance says: 'I don't want this.'

Acceptance says: 'OK, let's work with this.'

Resistance leads to stasis. Very often it consumes lots of energy to no purpose.

Acceptance enables you to build your ambition on a solid foundation and thus reach higher because it does not deny the reality of the situation. At the same time it does not mean you must 'suck up' and endure forever a situation that you dislike. It means accept the reality instead of fighting it – which is a natural but often futile reaction.

(You can fight the Internet if you want to, for example, but that goose is cooked, and the modern world depends on it.)

Say 'Yes, and... '

The people who really know how to build a big future based on whatever gets thrown at them are to be found in your local comedy theatre at an improv show (improvisation theatre, to give it it's proper name). If you've ever seen the TV series Whose Line Is It Anyway? then you know where we're going with this.

Dr Dolittle discovered the Pushmi-Pullyu, a distant relation of the Unicorn, Abyssinian Gazelle and Asiatic Chamois. The trouble is, if the Pushmi-Pullyu decisively wants to go one way then it most assuredly wants to go the other way. Going nowhere at a full gallop is the most likely outcome. Someone needs to take control.

Each actor has to build a story, spontaneously and unscripted based on information supplied by another performer or even shouted from the audience.

We, as members of the audience, gasp and very often cry laughing at the imagination, mental agility, creativity, speed of thought and the audacious shifts in narrative direction that performers achieve.

Life, after all is much like an improv show.

You don't know what will come at you or when.
But what you get is all you have to work with.

What you make of your future depends on what you can imagine
based on what you've got.

So how do they do it?

Acceptance.

No matter what absurd or lacklustre situation is presented, the
performer must build on it. It's an approach called 'Yes, and… '.

The US comedian, Stephen Colbert said:

> 'When I was starting out in Chicago, doing
> improvisational theatre with Second City and other
> places, there was really only one rule I was taught
> about improv. That was, "yes-and… "
>
> 'To build anything onstage, you have to accept what
> the other improviser initiates… . They say you're
> doctors – You're doctors!
>
> 'And then you add to that: We're doctors and we're
> trapped in an ice cave.
>
> 'That's the "-and"

And then hopefully they "yes-and" you back ...

You have to be aware of what the other performer is offering you, so that you can free and add to it. And through these agreements, you can improvise a scene or a one-act play ...

'Cynics always say no. But saying "yes"' begins things. Saying "yes" is how things grow. Saying "yes" leads to knowledge.'

Commencement speech by Stephen Colbert in 2006

In the film *Zoolander*, male models are being manipulated to assassinate world leaders. It turns out to be very easy to do this.

The plot is being explained to the world's leading male model Derek Zoolander. Playing to stereotype Zoolander is having the whole thing spelled out to him.

The actor, Ben Stiller, who is playing Zoolander forgets the line that follows the explanation so he improvises and repeats the question. This – and the improvised response by David Duchovny, who plays the hand model J.P. Prewitt, – reinforces the stereotype and adds to the story.

The scene goes like this

Zoolander: 'So why male models?'

Prewitt: 'Think about it Derek. Male models are genetically structured to be assassins. They're in peak physical condition. They can gain entry to the most secure places in the world. Most important of all: Models don't think for themselves. They DO AS THEY'RE TOLD!'

Zoolander: 'That is not true.'

Prewitt: 'Yes it is Derek!'

Zoolander: 'OK.'

Prewitt: 'Yeah – think about any photoshoot you have ever been in... '

Zoolander ponders then says: 'Good point.'

...A long and involved explanation of the fashion industry's involvement in syndicated crime and evil then follows. This is when Stiller forgets the scripted response. There's a pause, then he improvises and goes back to the opening line:

Zoolander: 'So why male models?'

Six long seconds of awkwardness follow...

Prewitt: 'Are you serious? I just told you that... A moment ago.'

Zoolander: 'Right... '.

It's much easier to say 'no'. Most of us are no-sayers. But we can train ourselves to be yes-sayers.

'Those who say "Yes" are rewarded by the adventures they have. Those who say "No" are rewarded by the safety they attain.' said Keith Johnstone in his book Impro.

In improv, resistance is called 'blocking', which means rejecting the reality provided to you. For example, a performer may begin

'We're sitting at the kitchen table' and you might say 'No. This isn't a kitchen, we're in a mucky cow shed.'

It might be funny for a moment. But blocking prevents a story evolving or thoughts developing and pretty fast you lose the engagement of the audience.

'Yes, but... '

This is just 'no' in disguise. Don't fall for it.

It's not 'yes, and... '

There are two components to 'Yes, and'.

'Yes-' >>>> Acceptance >>>> OMG the wifi is down

'and... ' >>>> Acting purposefully on this knowledge >>>> I'm going to read a book

'Yes... ' is acceptance

It's pretty hard to apply your energy to thinking big if you haven't accepted the reality of what it is you want to change or improve on. It's like trying to build a house on foundations that deep down you know do not exist. This isn't about being passive or helpless or putting up with crap. This is the sine qua non of thinking clearly.

As Carl Jung said: 'We cannot change anything until we accept it'.

But as soon as we do accept it we find that shifting from resistance to acceptance already starts making us change our perspective, our momentum, our intention and our thoughts get bigger.

As the psychologist Carl Rogers said: 'The curious paradox is that when I accept myself as I am, then I change.'

'...and' is going one step further

And one step further means spending more time developing your idea. It means fearlessly being creative, exploring your options, considering new directions of your company, your art, your personal journey.

'Yes, and' allows you to build on your situation whatever it might be. Even therapy.

The pioneering therapist Milton Erickson applied the 'yes and...' mentality to his work with patients. In a paper comparing improv with therapy, Earl Vickers referred to a time when a psychotic patient in the hospital came to Erickson and said 'I am Jesus Christ!'

The regular approach would be to explain why this was not the case. But, as the wit Clive James once observed: 'You cannot reason someone out of a position they did not reason themselves into in the first place.'

Creating resistance would not have achieved much.

Instead, Erickson replied 'I hear you know something about carpentry.'

Vickers wrote: 'Instead of directly contradicting the young man's delusions, thereby destroying the therapeutic opportunity, Erickson shifted him toward productive work by having him build a bookcase'.

One step ever further

There's more juice to be sucked out of 'Yes and... ' than acceptance and redirection of your thinking.

Think about the crazy stories that emerge from the development of an improv story line. Just when a story seems to have hit a dead end it gets funnier, more absurd, pivots and changes direction.

This is the alchemy of being pushed further than seemed possible.

> # 'Rarely have I seen a situation where doing less than the other guy is a good strategy.'
>
> *Jimmy Spithill, skipper of Team Oracle USA*

'Yes and... ', never saying no but always pushing further, is the difference between an amusing story and an outlandish hysterical one that comes from the speaker being forced to dig deeper into their resources than they thought they needed to or could do.

The performers themselves are regularly astounded at the stories they come up with, the memories they suddenly rediscover and harness.

Going one step ever further with your thoughts and with your efforts to make your thoughts actual – is a vital discipline in thinking big.

Thinking is hard work. The temptation is always to give up.

But thinking bigger is, by definition, going further than you normally do.

For you, one step further means hang on, ponder your fragile white horse of a thought a little bit longer, even though the effort of thinking makes you feel uncomfortable and want to let go.

It's like the physical trainer who makes you run ten metres further just when you thought you were done with your sprint.

It's why great painters forever paint over work that seems perfect to the rest of us. It's why historians of art find that beneath one famous painting lies another painting – or discover a figure that was painted over as the artist just kept pushing further and further.

Just when you want to stop is the moment that signals greatness around the corner. As the writer George Bernard Shaw said: 'Few people think more than two or three times a year; I have made an international reputation for myself by thinking once or twice a week.'

A similar process happens when entrepreneurs start working on their business idea.

Once you get that initial spark of a business idea – which might be a brand new product or the belief that there might be a better way to operate an industry, say, by making it easier for consumers to book travel tickets – then you need to go 'yes and...'.

 Sylvan Goldman owned the Piggly Wiggly supermarket chain in Oklahoma City and he was doing pretty well. But the amount he could sell to his customers was limited by the strength of their arm muscles and the pain in their fingers.

He mulled over the problem, which was that shoppers 'had a tendency to stop shopping when the baskets became too full or too heavy.'

Recruiting a carpenter and a maintenance man he put wheels on the legs of a folding chair and placed a basket on the seat; this ungainly contraption was the prototype for the first grocery cart.

But the idea didn't catch on; shoppers didn't want to use trolleys. Men felt it suggested they were too weak to carry their own shopping and mothers (at the time) felt as if they had already pushed enough prams in their lives.

Goldman's trolleys made perfect sense but that wasn't enough.

So he thought 'Yes and... ' and went the extra yard.

He hired assistants to offer carts to shoppers and brought in models to walk around his stores demonstrating by example how they could take their time, gather huge volumes of shopping and do so without breaking sweat or rupturing their biceps.

Eventually it took off, supermarkets were redesigned for trolley-shopping and Goldman was able to collect a royalty on every folding trolley sold.

Goldman had surfaced his white horse. And he went further and made his idea real. But it wasn't enough. He had to produce more good ideas to make his first good idea successful.

That's what it took: Ideas upon ideas, thinking big upon thinking big, to bring forth into the world his Big Idea, which would eventually not only make him a multi-millionaire but would also be one of those little noticed inventions that change the world.

These ideas, little kernels of thoughts, have to be beaten up, exposed to criticism, tested, reviewed, probed for commercial soundness and polished before people will want to risk using the product, investing in it, joining a team or leaving a good job to go full time.

This demands the 'Yes and...' habit to accept the reality, accept the feedback and turn that energy to your advantage.

Going one step further, sitting and simply thinking for one minute longer, can be the difference between letting the fragile butterfly of inspiration get away from you or capturing something special.

It's the difference between developing that white horse into something tangible or giving up and ending up in the same place tomorrow.

In other words putting in the effort is critical to avoiding Massive Monday.

Winners keep the ball in play

Tennis professionals win 80% of their points. Amateurs lose 80% of theirs.

What this means is that when professionals play each other the shot that wins the point, four fifths of the time, is so good that their opponent cannot return it.

When amateurs play, 80% of the points are scored because one of the players duffs the ball into the net, skies it out, double-faults, swipes-and-misses or trips over their laces.

Observing this, the physicist and author Simon Ramo explained that the way to win an amateur game was simply to keep the ball in play and let the other player lose.

This is harder than it sounds. And the discipline it takes is similar to that which you need to keep your energy focused on developing your big thoughts. Each time the challenge comes to you, you say "yes … and" you keep the game going.

The temptation to take wild swings for glory, to get a rush of blood to the head is enormous. In tennis, as in life, keeping focused on the prize of winning the match not merely the point takes constant reminding of what you're trying to do.

Just keep the ball in play. Keep the dream alive.

The tennis player who keeps the ball in play is taking the situation as it comes at her – however hard it is hit or with however much spin – and keeping the point going.

Yes is getting to the ball hit by your opponent.

And yes is keeping your focus on winning by keeping the ball in play rather than whipping an outrageous "hail mary" cross court backhand passing shot that also flies beyond the court and into the park beyond.

In the game of life And is just as hard as Yes.

Here are the times when you should take that one minute more:

When you have that wisp of an idea, of innovation or inspiration that hovers tantalizingly out of reach: don't pick up the phone. Don't do anything but this: think about it 30 seconds longer and then take 30 seconds to make a note of it. Try to tease it out. Because that idea will vanish no matter how confident you are that it will always be there.

When you've just been knocked back – by someone else's reaction to your ideas or even by your own self-doubt... pause. Don't abandon ship. Think about the number of times people have proved doubters wrong; consider all the life experience and passion that you bring to the table; consider all the things that brought your thinking to this point and what makes it valid and what part of the criticism is valid. Accept the revised reality – as Goldman did – and reject the bits which you can do without. Course-correct; keep moving.

After you've had a meeting: take one minute to write down the outtakes of the meeting. What were the moods of the participants, how do you feel about it, what was the learning, what's the most important thing coming from it? Just doing this will enable you to extract more value from every meeting you ever have.

'It is not always the people
who start out the smartest who
end up the smartest.'

Alfred Binet, the inventor of the IQ test

'When a distinguished but elderly
scientist states that something is
possible he is almost certainly right.

When he states that something is
impossible, he is very probably wrong.'

Arthur C. Clarke's advice about experts has become
known as Clarke's first law

HAVE A BIG EGO AND A SMALL EGO

Be an amateur

The awesome totality of the combined, accumulated, piled up and towering knowledge of the human race has established that we can say with great certainty that we cannot be sure about very much.

We have learned, for example, that so immense is the Universe that for every grain of sand on our planet there are about 10,000 stars.

> The world of the known is small and narrow and you already inhabit it.

Once you start thinking in those numbers it's pretty hard to be certain you know a fraction of anything.

Pretty much everything is unknown and truly this is a liberating thought for your personal ambition. Moving into the unknown is precisely what happens when you start thinking big.

In stark contrast, if you keep spiralling around the Massive Monday loop you are dealing very firmly in the world of the known. When it comes to Massive Monday most people are professionals. They've been there done that and they're going round again.

The world of the known is small and narrow and you already inhabit it.

The moment you start paying attention to your white horses and expanding your horizons you're crossing the threshold from pro to amateur.

Congratulations. This has a very proud tradition. Only amateurs ever discover new worlds and new horizons.

Scientists have a professional's discipline and rigour but an amateur's delight in pushing boundaries and discovering the unknown.

> The word Amateur derives from the Latin word Amare, which means 'to love'.
>
> This is appropriate. If you are going to bring this white horse into your life then you should be passionate about it.
>
> Ambition divorced from passion is a hollow shell.

'Science is the belief in the ignorance of experts.'

Richard Feynman

The 'scientific method' of thinking assumes no theory is ever right. The most you can scientifically state is that a theory has not yet been proven to be wrong. This is the basis of all science: that nothing is certain but that theories have yet to be revealed as wrong.

The point of all this is that uncertainty is a normal state for the people who are discovering the universe, life, themselves and their bigger horizons. You, too, can afford to be comfortable with it.

Amateurs have passion and ambition.

They've also got less to lose than experts. Experts have a vested interest in being at the top of any tower of knowledge or skill. They don't want their tower to be disrupted.

As you start pursuing the things you are interested in, as you start filling your mashup bag, and as you leave the reservation of the tried and tested, you are by definition an amateur.

This is the space where you take risks, you grow your ideas and indeed you grow as a person.

It's not just experts that might intimidate you as you enter the life-expanding world of the amateur. The same is true in the creative fields too.

Don't be fooled. Mistakes are made by everyone.

"Artists have a vested interest in our believing in the flash of revelation, the so-called inspiration...shining down from the heavens as a ray of grace", said the German philosopher Friedrich Nietzsche.

"In reality the imagination of the good artist or thinker produces continuously good, mediocre, or bad things, but his judgement, trained and sharpened to a fine point, rejects, selects, connects... All great artists and thinkers are great workers, indefatigable not only in inventing but also in rejecting, sifting, transforming and ordering."

AMATEUR -v- PRO

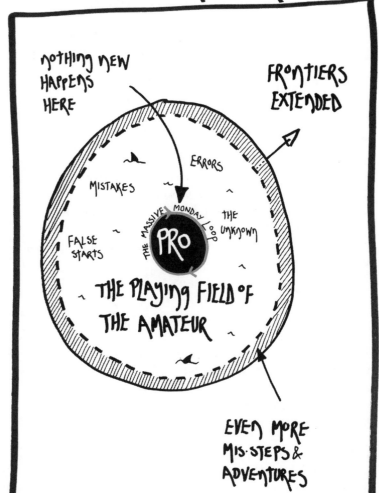

nothing new
happens
here

FRONTIERS
EXTENDED

ERRORS

MISTAKES

FALSE
STARTS

THE MASSIVE MONDAY LOOP

PRO

THE
UNKNOWN

THE PLAYING FIELD OF
THE AMATEUR

EVEN MORE
MIS·STEPS &
ADVENTURES

Seek mountains and obstacles

The pursuit of a bigger life throws up all sorts of obstacles. That's natural. In fact, if you see obstacles you are on the right track.

If you make mistakes on your journey then learn from them.

'The departure point for inspiration is the obstacle.'

Gianfranco Contini.

We are taught to hate losing arguments and making mistakes but that is small thinking. The sort of person who can appreciate how such 'set backs' can drive progress is onto something. With each set back they learn more, expand their horizons, redirect their ambition and keep on embracing life. It's exactly the sort of person that Google looks to hire.

What does Google search for?

What Google looks for in its new hires is 'intellectual humility'.

The company has learned that graduates from the top business schools plateau. Someone whose life is a dizzy haze of dazzling academic success, trouncing tests and exam ecstasy is pretty unaccustomed to failure. So they don't learn how to unwrap the gift of learning that failure offers.

Instead, as they swish through life, they attribute all success to their personal genius and attach all failures to the actions, inactions or idiocy of others.

'The people who are the most successful here, who we want to hire, will have a fierce position', said Laszlo Bock, in an interview with

The New York Times. Bock is the Senior Vice President of People Operations at Google.

'They'll argue like hell. They'll be zealots about their point of view. But then you say "here's a new fact" and they'll go "Oh, well that changes things; You're right".'

How does Bock describe the sort of person who can be passionate about their ideas but prepared to admit they are wrong?

'You need a big ego and a small ego in the same person at the same time.'

The ambition of amateurs

Lord Kelvin, one of the great and most farsighted physicists of the nineteenth century thought the idea of flying was absurd. He said: 'heavier than air flying machines were impossible'. This was the prevailing view.

Only a very few people dared dream bigger than this. They were all amateurs. After all there could be no experts in something that had never been done before.

The sceptics were famously proved wrong by the bicycle mechanics known as the Wright Brothers.

Notably, it was not just the dominant thinking that was proved wrong.

In 1901 Wilbur Wright said to his brother that 'man would not fly for fifty years.'

Nevertheless he and Orville wrestled with their white horse, they went the extra yard, they learned everything they could, they mashed up their bicycle mechanics' skills with theorizing about aeronautics.

And two years later, not 50 years later, they launched an airplane from Kitty Hawk. And the rest as they say, is vapour trails.

Fight your corner

Heisenberg's uncertainty principle states that something can be in one place at the same time that it's in another place.

This pretty much describes how you reconcile your big ego of passion and ambition with your small ego – your humility.

The point is that having intellectual humility – accepting you are an amateur and could be wrong – does not absolve you from fiercely defending your position for so long as you believe in it.

It takes guts to accept you're wrong. But it also takes guts to stick up for your position, your opinion and your ambition. Stand up for what you believe in and what you have created.

Have the courage to make your case and the humility to accept when you are wrong.

You are a born optimist

Fear and optimism circle each other like two pouting tango dancers.

These two emotional states are oppositional. But it is the magic of the two together that leads us forward.

Fear signposts the way beyond the comfort zone. It makes you anxious and hesitant about your new venture and your ambition but it is optimism which urges you onward. When optimism conquers fear, then you progress.

In this way optimism changes your future. This is no fluke.

Our natural evolution-developed neurological bias is to be optimists. And optimism acts like a giant planet in the universe of our lives. It has gravitational heft; it's a heavy mass that pulls and warps reality in our favour.

Our optimism changes our objective reality – the way things really are – and transforms it into the shape of our dreams. It's a powerful force.

Consider this. Optimists are likely to believe they will live longer than average and as a result are demonstrably proven to save more, take more vitamins, eat healthier, exercise more and have a sunnier disposition. And indeed optimists do live longer, are less stressed and healthier.

Several studies have demonstrated that an optimistic attitude is a more accurate indicator of someone's likelihood of surviving certain cancers than size of tumour or the patient's age.

Meanwhile some research suggests that those with a cynical disposition are more likely to develop dementia. If this is the case – and it's early days in the study – then it might be due to the extra effort of considering the downside of everything and everyone.

Which is a timely reminder of this: you are what you are thinking all day.

The 'let's fix this' attitude

If you expect positive outcomes then your response to setbacks is healthier. It's not that setbacks won't happen. Of course they will. Especially if you are extending your amateurishness.

But when things go wrong – your inventive dinner party is a disaster, you do worse than you expect on a test, no-one visits your website – then the important thing is what happens next.

If you are a pessimist, then when things go wrong your response is 'oh great, situation normal'. You have less inclination to ask 'why' questions and consequently it is unlikely you'll do better next time. If you even pursue a next time.

Brain scans have shown that when optimists make mistakes activity flares in an area of the brain which processes self-reflection and recollection. But in pessimists this area of the brain shows no heightened activity when they make mistakes.

Who makes the most accurate predictions

Severe depression → expect things to be worse than they end up being.
Mild depression → pretty accurate expectation of the future.
Optimist → expect the future to be better than it ends up being.

'Optimism is denying reality'.

Ajit Varki, University of California, San Diego

Optimists and pessimists

Optimists and pessimists share the same probability of getting divorced.

Optimists are more likely to get remarried.
(Study from Duke University)

What this suggests is that upon failing a task the optimist's brain says: 'Woah! What just happened?' And this, of course, is the precursor to working out what went wrong and saying: 'Let's fix this'.

Inside the pessimist the activity in this part of the brain simply flat lines. It indicates that no reflection goes on. Pessimism encourages passive acceptance of bad news rather than striving to conquer it and make the objective reality fit our ambitious expectations.

The pessimist unsurprisingly, doesn't change their world for the better, for as you know: The mind leads and life follows.

Startup optimists

Only a masochist would set up their own business. Take it from me I do it regularly.

But each time I know it will do better.

'Hold on, let's fix this!' is the mentality of the growing number of startup business founders. The likelihood that any of them will be the next Google or Facebook is outrageously low. But every founder believes that they will confound the statistics and convert their business into a great success.

If the business doesn't get the user numbers they hoped for, if they don't get onto the accelerator programme they applied to, they don't get the investment they feel they justified, or their partners turn out to be snakes then they go harder next time. They remain optimists, and this disposition – this belief that they can warp reality to their shiny expectation – enables them to summon up more white horses.

How optimism helps us cope with a very big thought

The bias towards optimism is critical to survival. Tali Sharot, author of *The Optimism Bias*, wrote that it's what 'keeps us moving forward rather than to the nearest high-rise ledge. Without optimism, our ancestors might never have ventured far from their tribes and we might all be cave dwellers, still huddled together and dreaming of light and heat.'

Here's where optimism really kicks in. We take for granted the amazing gift of mental time travel. We can travel both directions, we can imagine the future – our summer holiday – and we can compare it to our past – the vacation last year.

This enables ambition, careers, saving for a rainy day, plotting world domination and drooling over an amazing dinner last week. But the crux of the thing is that time travel could cripple us. It brings with it a shuddering truth. Our ability to skip back and forth ends ultimately with the knowledge of our own mortality.

This knowledge ought to be so devastating that no caveman would ever leave the cave. Like Marvin the severely depressed, paranoid android from *The Hitchhiker's Guide to the Galaxy*, this knowledge bears down on us and forces the question: what's the point?

It is our inbuilt bias to be optimistic that allows us to park this thought and marvel at the miracle of life. The scientist Ajit Varki, at the University of California, San Diego, argues that this is the power of denial or 'mind over reality'.

The likelihood is that optimism evolved hand-in-hand with our ability to time travel, he says.

Without this ability to block out fears and bad outcomes we would not strap ourselves to rockets and fly to the moon, drive fast cars, continue to eat oysters, learn about the Universe or gasp in wonderment at the world we inhabit.

'When there's a tornado in the Midwest', Varki points out, 'all the animals disappear 10 to 15 minutes early; all the humans come out to watch.'

Tornado gazing

This is the spirit of thinking big. Not paralysed and wailing about the shortness of our mortal coil but seizing and running with the potential of life.

'Sometimes I sits and thinks.

Sometimes I just sits.'

Winnie the Pooh

KNOW YOUR WEAPON

Stacking and flowing

Famously, the Eskimos have a zillion words for snow.

It makes sense. If something plays a big role in your life then it helps to understand its every aspect and nuance, every flake and crystal. So to speak.

In England we have more words for rain than, say, the desert people of the world.

Words like spitting, drizzle, April showers, pouring, cats and dogs, stair rods, bucketing down, misty rain, barely raining, call-this-rain?, steady rain, torrential and biblical all help us know how wet we're going to get on the way to work.

And they help us dress appropriately for picnics and Glastonbury.

So it's peculiar that in general day-to-day use, we only have one word for the thing that we do all day long: thinking. In fact it's more than odd. It's deeply unhelpful. It needs fixing.

Neither you nor I shall become Eskimos of the brain in one short book. But we can introduce some helpful concepts that will allow us to think bigger, better.

There are as many ways to think about thinking as there are neuroscientists. Fortunately, you just need two.

You need to know when to pay concentrated attention to a matter and when to let go and allow the magic subconscious to do its thing.

Your big ideas – your white horses – come from a blend of both. It's partly unbidden inspiration and passion. And it's partly methodically working through the stages to make the dream real.

Most big ideas need a blend of the two.

They are called stacking and flowing.

These are your weapons against Massive Monday, the Sargasso Sea of the mind and sea squirt-drifting.

Simply knowing whether your mind is stacking or flowing, or which is needed to address a particular problem, or stage of a challenge, will help you think bigger.

One of the fastest growing bodies of human knowledge is neuroscience. The things that the brilliant men and women in neuroscience labs around the world are discovering will boggle your brain. Literally.

For example, if you apply electro-magnetic energy to the correct part of your brain through the use of a (kind of) carefully calibrated cattle prod, then the subject can become more creative, intelligent or dumb temporarily.

(Scientists usually experiment on students, not each other.)

This is fascinating. But to you and me, this is as useful as a one-legged man in an ass-kicking contest.

This is not to say for a moment that neuroscience isn't important or enlightening. But for the most part the knowledge isn't usable by people wanting to make change in their real life right this instant.

Our focus is to keep it simple and usable.

A ZILLION WORDS FOR THIS

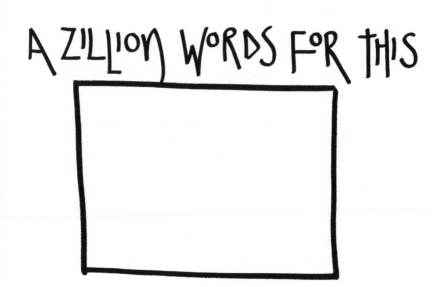

ONLY ONE WORD FOR THIS

Know your tools and when to use them.

Now, I know your brain is a marvel of the universe but for a moment think of it like a humble paddle. If you are making your way across the Amazon rain forest by foot and by canoe then the paddle is at some moments your vital means of propulsion. Once you reach land the paddle transforms all of a sudden into a burden but your legs have just as suddenly become useful. Hopefully you'll recognize when to use your legs and when to use your paddle.

The moral is: know your tools and when to use them.

Stacking is analytical and logic-driven. It progresses incrementally. It is focused and directed activity; directed towards a specific purpose which you will reach gradually through the power of sitting on your backside (usually) and applying your mind to the problem.

It may not be easy and requires grit and determination; but you know what you're doing and roughly how you're going to do it. Like building a little stack of bricks, you get there step by step.

Since the days of Aristotle the logical and analytical approach has been the 'go to' way of handling most intellectual challenges and it's how we manage most day to day tasks.

On the other hand when your mind is flowing it will go where it will.

The direction of the flow cannot be precisely targeted or the force of it carefully calibrated.

Flowing is the state of day dreaming and pondering. It's present in the wandering thoughts that produce a sudden insight – an epiphany – the magical moment when all at once you solve a problem that seemed impossible only moments before.

It's a huge contrast in state of mind. When you're stacking, you advance one brick at a time; but when you're flowing you are probably lost at sea right up to the point that you find yourself sitting in your hotel bedroom with the answer safely tucked in the pocket of your fluffy dressing gown.

What's going on in these two different states of mind, what are they good for and how does knowing about them make life any better?

A good place to start is the eyes.

Focused eyes

Typical stacking tasks are trying to balance the books, writing a report, analysing data, planning a picnic (in the barely raining rain), writing most computer code. The solution won't be a sudden breakthrough but comes from methodical thinking, like a train pulling carriages along fixed tracks.

Sometimes it's a process of elimination such as: 'We can't serve fish because Jon is a vegetarian and we can't serve peanuts because Jen has an allergy, plus we have a budget of £20 and we need to fit it all in a cooler.'

When your mind is stacking you can sense when you are making progress. According to psychological studies when you are solving a problem through logic you can actually sense yourself getting closer. You have a 'feeling of knowing'.

Stacking is also known as 'convergent thinking', because all your powers of concentration converge on the problem.

When you're deeply immersed in this sort of problem solving your pupils dilate.

They get larger because concentration is active in the front part of your brain where the visual processing occurs. Think about the language we use: we talk of the problem being the one we're 'looking at now'.

It's no surprise that we call this state of mind focused.

Predatory animals, like a cat, are utterly consumed with their prey when they are stalking something.

In fact, if you've ever seen a Gundog like a Pointer focused on its target you will see the entire being of the animal, every fibre, sinew and synapse is charged and zeroed in on the prey. Its mind is definitely not flowing where it will. It is utterly focused and converging its energy on the target.

Unfocused eyes

Logic, analysis and determination will get you a long way. But when you need fresh ideas or a new perspective you need to use your mind in a different way.

And you may want to blur your eyes – which is clearly not the sort of thing you do when you're on the hunt.

When your mind is in a state of flow, thoughts and connections are free to roam. Your subconscious matches all sorts of combinations of ideas in a playful, light-hearted way. Some of these ideas surface in our consciousness but most probably do not.

The more you have stuffed into your mashup bag the more combinations can be brought together.

And suddenly while you may not have been aware you were even thinking about it you solve a problem: like understanding the odd behaviour of a colleague, realizing why the books don't balance, creating a new product innovation, inventing a new design approach or stumbling on the general theory of relativity.

When you have such a sudden and inexplicable flash of insight, your brain 'blinks'.

At this moment your mind is not focused on what is in front of it but it is travelling the infinite possibilities of its own synapses. Just before the epiphany surfaces the right visual cortex shows the same activity (under a brain scanner) as it does when you close your eyes.

In other words, even if your eyes are open, the brain appears to shut off vision momentarily.

You may have noticed that when people are asked a question which requires them to use their imagination or their memory, very often they close their eyes – they physically (but involuntarily) stop processing vision.

The answers – it turns out – are inside you.

WHEN CLOSED, YOUR EYES TURN INWARD AND GAZE AT THE INFINITY OF YOUR IMAGINATION

Passing the parcel

As you think your way past problems and towards success you'll need to constantly switch between stacking and flowing. Which you do first depends on where you are with your problem solving.

Whereas your imagination is let loose by flowing, the act of creativity usually requires you to convert the imagined ideas into something concrete and this requires logical, methodical activity. Or it may be that you need to do some hard stacking to really understand the obstacles that the subconscious flows through while you're taking a walk.

And if, then, an idea for a beautiful dress design comes to you from a flowing insight while walking back from lunch then it will be the methodical side of your thinking that you use to work out how to make it real.

From flowing to stacking

Einstein explained that at his most creative he used mental images, symbols and signs.

The images would contain meaning and logic. But to achieve greater insights and bigger thoughts he would not use language because this would switch his mind into a logical mode and this would stifle the breadth of his creativity.

He would play with these ideas and concepts, match them with each other, explore and test, until he felt he had a great feel for his insight. When he reached the point where he was ready to articulate the logic of his thoughts in words he would switch from flowing to stacking.

He explained that: 'Conventional words or other signs have to be sought for laboriously only in a second stage, when the ... associative play is sufficiently established and can be reproduced at will.'

From stacking to flowing

Here's an example of the opposite sequence of activity.

Scientists typically use a type of text called a RAT (Remote Association Test) to examine how people are approaching problem solving and creativity.

The challenge is to find a word which combines meaningfully with a triad of words that the examiner gives you. A typical triad would be 'falling, dust, rock' or 'notch, flight, spin'.

The word that combines with each of the words in the first triad is 'star' and the second set would be linked by the word 'top'.

When someone stares at the words on the paper with focus and intent then they are stacking, going through words that might fit by systematically testing them against each part of the triad. This may or may not produce the answer.

If it doesn't then the subject might blink or look away from the words. This is when they begin flowing and thinking abstractly.

What this simple experiment shows is how flowing follows stacking. Subjects couldn't usefully start letting their minds flow before they had primed them by really studying the problem hard and familiarizing themselves with the challenge.

The importance of time of day

Intriguingly, there are times of day when it's better to stack and others when it's best to flow. What those times are depends on whether you're a night owl or up with the lark.

Your self-discipline and your inhibitions are at their weakest when you're tired and groggy. This self-discipline is what you need when you're stacking.

It's what keeps you rooted to your seat as you grind your way through a problem or plot how to turn your grand ambition into vibrant reality.

The self-discipline allows for peak concentration and you need this to filter out the distractions of the world.

When you're flowing, however, you want to take the mental shackles off. Creativity peaks when you're tired (and so does unethical behaviour which is why it's harder to resist the cookie jar when you're feeling sleepy).

And so, if you're a morning person you're likely to have strong will power and be awesome at mental stacking early in the day. This may wear off as the day progresses and as night time approaches and sleepiness encroaches your self-discipline slides, your creativity starts to let go, your imagination lets slip its bindings and your thinking may start to 'embiggen'. This is when insights, solutions and your authentic voice seem to surface like magic.

On the other hand night owls may inhabit a semi-dream state when they first wake up. As my friends, family and business colleagues know this is how I am before noon. But it's the best time of day to flow. The discipline to get things done comes later in the day for me. During the morning I am a day dreamer. This is common for night owls.

Knowing this enables me to be more effective with planning my time. You will work out what's best for you simply by being aware of these different modes of thinking and seeing when your ability for each peaks.

'No matter where you go;
there you are.'

Confucius

'Ask a toad what is beauty ...
he will answer that it is a female with
two great round eyes coming out of
her little head, a large flat mouth,
a yellow belly and a brown back.'

Voltaire

'If we were orcs, wouldn't we
at a racial level, IMAGINE
ourselves to look like elves?'

Oscar Wao – whose mind constantly drifted to fantasy stories such as
Lord of the Rings – thinking about how beauty is in the (prejudiced)
eye of the beholder.

Junot Diaz, *The Brief Wondrous Life of Oscar Wao*

TRAVEL LIGHT

Check your assumptions

There's a big, strong mother elephant and there's a baby elephant.

The baby elephant is tied to a post by a thick rope. It strains and heaves against the rope trying to break free.

The mother elephant is tied to a post by a thin, fraying rope. With her enormous strength she could snap the rope or uproot the post. She does neither.

A child observes this and scratches her head. She speaks to the elephant trainer.

'The baby cannot escape but tries to. The mother can escape but does not', she says. 'Why doesn't the mother break free?'

'When she was a baby she also tried to break free. She learned that she could not', he replies. 'Now she assumes it is still impossible. She is tied by the strongest rope of all.'

> ## 'For people to accept the yoke, they must believe they have no choice.'
>
> *Michael Lewis, Liar's Poker*

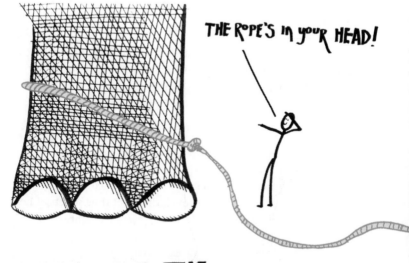

TIED BY THE
STRONGEST ROPE OF ALL

Your mind is an incredible tool. Your goal is to unlock its potential to think bigger.

But while you have been purposefully or aimlessly travelling the ocean of life (and loitering in the vortex of garbage) your mind has picked up a lot of baggage that weighs down and cramps your thinking.

This sack of rocks inside your head is strangely difficult to notice. Seek to be aware of the way your thinking is constrained by the biases and prejudices you bring with you.

As a law-abiding, queue-trained Brit I was surprised when my South African friend, driving through the night time streets of her home town, Cape Town, cruised through every red light.

'Oh, they're just suggestions', she explained.

And this is true. Just like the dashed lines in the middle of the road. We can ignore them if we want. We choose to take notice. No red light can physically make you stop your car (although I imagine Google has plans for this). Nor can a green light make your foot hit the gas.

These are rules we make for ourselves and we agree to conform to as part of a social contract. They vary from culture to culture. If a passenger refuses to wear a seatbelt in some countries they will offend the law-abiding driver. If the passenger wears a seat belt in other countries the law-abiding driver will also be offended at the implied insult.

Beware the baggage you project onto the world

I want to talk about The Dude. The Dude learned how much of the world was real and how much was just the biases and interpretations and bag of rocks that he projected on to it.

You know who the Dude is, right? The Dude is Lebowski.

The Big Lebowski is probably the most celebrated of the very many films made by Jeff Bridges. His character, The Dude reflects much of the Zen philosophy that Bridges actually practices and has written about.

Not surprisingly, the character and the actor often get conflated.

So here we are. Now Jeff Bridges climbs into an isolation tank.

An isolation tank is a large soundproof, lightproof capsule containing water which is maintained at body temperature and is saturated with about 100 pounds of salt so that you can float.

He lies in this and he has no external sensations – no physical pressure, no visual stimuli, no sounds, just weightless, emptiness.

All he can hear is his body; his breathing, his heart beating.

Isolated in such a tank there is just you and your wandering mind.

> 'I wondered what I could think about and then realised I could just watch what was happening. I noticed my breathing. I noticed how much mental energy and thoughts I was producing in the tank even when the outside world didn't engage with me at all. In fact, I could almost see my mind as some kind of screen with thoughts and images projected on it. I also began to appreciate the power of my own intention to

somehow control these projections.

'I was in there for three hours. When I came out all the colours and sounds rushed in. I sensed them as never before, appreciating their richness and beauty. I also realised that the projections of my mind, so clear to me inside the tank, were continuing to be projected outside the tank. But outside the tank the blankness, emptiness was missing. Instead my projections were being cast on everything that my senses were receiving, so it was less apparent that so much information I had about them was actually coming from inside me. This was a very helpful bit of knowledge and very useful in my life.'

The immersion tank enabled The Dude to see what was objective reality and what was the subjective reality he projected onto the world.

As Anais Nin said: 'We don't see things as they are. We see them as we are.'

Beware the baggage of consistency

A child declares one day that he wants to be a train driver.

A week later he decides to be a spaceman. Then flirts with the idea of being a soldier. Then a rock star. Then a farmer, a painter, a footballer, a parachutist, a nurse, a cameraman, a lorry driver, a lego assembler and within a few years most occupations have been tried on for size. As a child tests these dreams some take a mental and emotional hold for a while and some don't.

Adults tend to be more serious. We feel we need to be consistent. Being solid and reliable in our dreams and aspirations is what we feel is expected of us.

CHILDREN GAZE UPON THE WIDE HORIZON

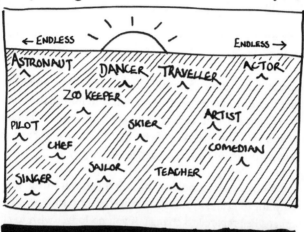

← ENDLESS   ENDLESS →

ASTRONAUT   DANCER   TRAVELLER   ACTOR
ZOO KEEPER
PILOT   SKIER   ARTIST
   CHEF   COMEDIAN
SINGER   SAILOR   TEACHER

ALL THERE IS
(YOU THINK)

ADULTS THINK THEY CAN SEE BETTER, LITTLE NOTICING HOW THEIR BAGGAGE OBSCURES THE VIEW

Ignore this consistency. It imposes a narrowness of thinking which is the mental equivalent of the hideous bindings which Chinese aristocrats used to tie around rich girls' feet in order that, as they grew up, their feet stayed petite and conformed with a prevailing idea of beauty.

It is not consistency itself that is bad. If you are consistent to your true north – your real ambition and dreams – then that is genuine.

The point is that you are constantly developing. As you travel from one shore of life to the other you pick up information, your personality changes, you learn things and you become a different person. And with the fast pace of change in technology, business and society the rate of personal change is ever greater.

This may subtly or profoundly change what you want from life; or how you want to express yourself through art or business. When this happens be prepared to change. If you no longer wish to climb the corporate ladder because you want more time or independence, or you no longer want to spend all your time training for triathlons because you have discovered, say, reading and photography –if this has happened and your ambitions have changed – then accept it.

Pretending you want something you no longer want, merely because you desire to appear consistent in the eyes of the world around you will cause you tremendous psychological pain.

Ignore the manual

There are three documented uses for top-loading washing machines in India. Only one of them is hidebound by the baggage of following the rules. The other two demonstrate a determination not to be shackled by small thinking.

1. Washing clothes.

2. Storing dry goods in a safe clean container when there is insufficient running water to wash clothes.

3. Stirring curd and making buttermilk or lassis. Washing machines are cheaper and more efficient than dedicated equipment.

Joseph Barrios, a cook had been shot in the head during a holdup. Doctors had saved his life but were concerned that the bullet, which they had not been able to extract, could move into a part of his brain that would be fatal.

The bullet was inaccessible through surgery.

So the doctors threw away their baggage of normal thinking. And they used their mashup bag of ideas.

Barrios was taken to a NASA centrifuge – a sort of whirligig which is used to train astronauts for the immense gravitational force of flying into space by spinning them round and round.

Barrios was spun around at six times the force of gravity to shift the bullet from the dangerous part of the brain to a safer part. The doctors were in the end unable to extract the bullet but said it had lodged in a soft tissue part of the brain where it would be encapsulated in scar tissue and rendered harmless for the rest of his life.

'He's as happy as can be', said the doctor of the man with a bullet in his brain.

The hot dog champ of thinking big

To travel light and set new limits the first thing you have to do is 'see the baggage'.

This is what the slight figure of Takeru Kobayashi did when he smashed the world record for competitive hot dog eating.

The standing record was 25 and 1/8 hot dogs in 12 minutes. Kobayashi, who weighs just over 9 stone was laughed at by fellow competitors at the Coney Island hot dog eating contest for being so puny.

Then he ate 50.

So comprehensive was his demolition of the previous record that the 'urban dictionary' says that to be a Kobayashi of something is to be the dominant player. Tiger Woods was once the Kobayashi of golf, for example.

But let's get back to the point. Kobayashi thought that the standing record shouldn't be the limit for his ambition because it would fence in his imagination of the possible. The previous contestants were carrying too much baggage: they thought 25 and 1/8 and possibly a fraction more was a true limit to the possible.

In fact they had hit a mental barrier not a physical barrier because they failed to think big about how to smash the record.

Speaking to Stephen Dubner on the Freakonomics podcast, Kobayashi said: 'I think the thing about human beings is that they make a limit in their mind of what their potential is and they decide that, "well, I have been told this or this is what society tells me".'

So Kobayashi approached the competition with fresh thinking. He worked out that it was more efficient to separate the frankfurters from the bread rolls. This is called the Solomon method.

While he started eating the frankfurters two at a time he dealt with the tricky problem of the buns.

To consume buns at pace he dunked them in a tumbler of water and then smushed them into his mouth. This makes them less dry – faster to chew and digest, and saves water-drinking time.

He also developed the 'Kobayashi Shake' which involves jumping up and down and twisting your torso which speeds food down your oesophagus and creates more stomach space.

So the question this leaves us with is this: is Kobayashi a one-off physical marvel or did he spot the mental baggage that everyone else was carrying too?

Well, you know the answer to this. Once Kobayashi showed the world their own baggage everyone dealt with it. They realized they had set limits on their own ambition. Joey Chestnut now holds the work record of 69.

These limits are everywhere. This is the mental baggage that holds back our ambition.

'... so if every human being actually threw away those thoughts and they actually did use that method of thinking to everything, the potential of human beings I think is really great, it's huge compared to what they think of themselves.' Kobayashi said to Dubner.

ADVICE FROM A TWO-FACED FRIEND

You might see a young woman with her face turned away from you or you might see the profile of an older lady with a hook nose and a wart. Whichever image you see first will be the baggage that makes it harder to see the other interpretation.

Noticing different options, considering different routes to take and weighing up alternative opinions is hard work.

"When the mind has seized on one view, it's amazingly difficult to get it to switch one's perception to see it from another point of view", said the designer Alan Fletcher*.

*This drawing is based on a sketch by Fletcher.

Tips for seeing clearly

When you're faced with an intractable problem or you need a new perspective here are some tools worth trying.

 ## Be someone else

Ask yourself how someone you admire (or even someone you dislike!) might approach a situation. How would Google/Apple/Steve Jobs/Vito Corleone tackle this problem.

'What Would Jesus Do?' became such a well-known thinking tool that WWJD was a bumper sticker seen across the US in the 1990s.

I prefer the secular, specific proposal of the writer Neil Gaiman: pretend you are a wise person.

What makes this mental exercise so effective is that putting yourself in someone else's shoes frees you of a lot of your own baggage because you try to saddle yourself with theirs!

 ## Be somewhere else

Distance matters.

The greater the imagined distance between you and an idea the more likely you will be able to critically evaluate it. As something gets closer people tend to become less interested in the concept and focus more on the practical problems such an idea might face.

When assessing ideas for a new business, a study by Jennifer Mueller showed that people tended to be far more critical when the person with the idea was said to be based around the corner than if the idea seems to come from a far distant source.

The moral is that to think critically about big concepts it helps to imagine some distance between you and the idea.

 ## Speak in a different language

The relationship between distance and bolder, more conceptual thinking manifests itself in other ways too. Take language. You will think more conceptually in another language than your mother tongue.

Bjork, the Icelandic music megastar, told The Guardian: '[speaking] English for me is still like an arm's length removed. You are always a bit different in the mother tongue. That's why it's maybe easier for me in English to be an extrovert. In Icelandic I'm more private.'

Bjork attended the Cannes film festival dressed as a swan.

 ## Treat your opinions like fair-weather friends

Your best opinions are those you hold in low regard.

Only such humble opinions will always be whittled and moulded to accurately fit the facts as you know them.

If you are happy to discard your opinions then, when new facts come to light, you are prepared to change your mind, and in that way your thinking remains the best it can be.

On the other hand, if your opinions are too important to your sense of self to dare change them, if you must resist and defend every argument no matter what the facts are, or what the reasoning is, then you may not learn much that is new.

In a world that changes as fast as ours, this is a self-defeating stance to take.

You might be right when you form your opinion. You might be wrong by the time you defend it to the death.

'Leave the world more interesting
for your being here.'

Neil Gaiman

...TWANG!

It don't mean a thing if it ain't got that twang

To make change, an idea must twang.

Place two guitars next to each other.

Pluck the D-string of one guitar and the D-string of the second guitar will also twang. Fundamental frequency is what makes this happen. The energy of one string matches the energy of the other and it creates a sympathetic vibration – it twangs. None of the other strings vibrate.

To coin a phrase, it strikes a chord.

This is resonance.

When you've nailed it, thinking big twangs. That's when your intention gets activated. It's when the scale of your thinking starts changing your reality.

First, it twangs for you – which means that deep in your core you truly believe in and are driven by your dreams and ambitions. They become your true north. If, say, your ambition is to eat more hot dogs in ten minutes than anyone on Earth only you know whether you really mean to do it.

Second, it twangs for others. When you tell your story, express your ambition or show your art then you want to create an emotional connection with your friends, your customers, readers, family or colleagues. You want them to be moved. You want them to support you or get out of the way.

When it twangs for you

Before you start acting on all this you probably have a few conditions you want satisfied. You might not have thought about this explicitly. But you'll remain sceptical unless it meets the conditions of what you might call 'human resonance':

1) You're convinced that your ambition truly reflects what you want, that it is authentically yours.

2) That it is grounded in the reality of your life but not limited by today's situation.

3) That you can take practical steps, no matter how small, in the right direction amid the daily rush of life.

If these boxes can't be checked then the idea may clang loudly – as noisily as a three year old with a tin drum – but it won't resonate. Clanging ain't twanging. It'll be an F-string to your A-string.

You will be unchanged.

But, if the idea meets these rules then you are going somewhere. And you are bringing your white horse back to shore.

When it twangs for others

When your idea twangs for others you make change. Your idea may start relatively small in the grand scheme of things. But so long as it connects with people then it can grow and you'll find that little things can make big change. It's the principle of the snowball which begins the size of your hand and rolls into a snow man and then an avalanche that clears every obstacle out of your way.

And this is also the magic of the 'trim tab' – a tiny mechanical device can have a disproportionate effect. It was famously described by R. Buckminster Fuller. In an interview with *Playboy* he said:

'Something hit me very hard once, thinking about what one little man could do. Think of the Queen Mary – the whole ship goes by and then comes the rudder. And there's a tiny thing at the edge of the rudder called a trim tab.

'It's a miniature rudder. Just moving the little trim tab builds a low pressure that pulls the rudder around. Takes almost no effort at all. So I said that the little individual can be a trimtab. Society thinks it's going right by you, that it's left you altogether. But if you're doing dynamic things mentally, the fact is that you can just put your foot out like that and the whole big ship of state is going to go.'

Spread the word

To make an emotional connection with your thinking you must become a story teller. Telling the story of your idea is the surest test of its value. If you can communicate your thinking in such simple words that your audience completely understand it and embrace it then you are really onto something.

> When the audience doesn't understand you, then probably you don't either.

If you start retreating into jargon and your audience begin scratching their heads and scrunching their faces as if they think they might sorta, kinda get it then, friend, you need to keep working on it.

In other words, if your idea doesn't survive contact with an audience then it isn't robust yet. When the audience doesn't understand you, then probably you don't either. It's not the end. But you have work to do.

Richard Feynman's colleague wrote: 'Feynman was a truly great teacher. He prided himself on being able to devise ways to explain even the most profound ideas to beginning students.

Once, I said to him, "Dick, explain to me, so that I can understand it, why spin one-half particles obey Fermi-Dirac statistics*."

Sizing up his audience perfectly, Feynman said, "I'll prepare a freshman lecture on it."

But he came back a few days later to say, "I couldn't do it. I couldn't reduce it to the freshman level. That means we don't really understand it."'

Coal miners used to take canaries into the tunnels. The canaries would sing when the air was safe. As soon as the singing stopped the miners knew that the air was getting unhealthy.

When you share your ideas you're looking for an opposite reaction. As soon as your audience get your idea then they'll be like the canaries that start singing. That's how you'll know you're twanging.

---

* Fermi-Dirac statistics? Don't ask. Because physics.

Being vulnerable

Sharing your ambition, telling people what you're thinking big about, and what you intend to do to make it happen means making yourself vulnerable in a way that you don't do when you're simply repeating what everyone else does and believes (or says they believe because life seems easier that way – just less like life).

Abandoning the herd, explaining why you're leaving the zoo, to become an outsider is bound to attract critics and trolls.

This makes it harder to tell your personal story, but you must. This is, after all, your personal journey.

This wave that has rolled across the sea of your life and which has culminated in your white horse is intrinsically the product of your experiences. It is how you got to this point that people want to hear. This is what makes it relevant, pertinent, valuable, interesting, emotional, valid.

Sharing your thinking exposes your personal journey to scrutiny but this is what the people want to hear.

Roll up!

'When you are a Bear of Very Little
Brain, and you Think of Things, you
find sometimes that a Thing which
seemed very Thingish inside you
is quite different when it gets out
into the open and has other people
looking at it.'

Winnie the Pooh

Saving lives and changing the world

They called it 'the suicide ward'. In the 1890s, the lower East Side of New York was one of the most densely populated square miles in the world. One third of children born there died before they reached the age of five.

The photo essayist Jacob Riis described it 'as a world of bad smells, scooting rats, ash barrels, dead goats and little boys drinking beer out of milk cartons'.

The newly-arrived immigrants from European farming villages, where someone might only meet a few hundred people in a lifetime, found themselves in city blocks where thousands lived. They had no idea how to cope with the 'crowd diseases' of measles, dysentry, typhoid, diphtheria and trachoma.

Diseases swept through families, tenement blocks, and communities killing thousands at a time.

Orthodox thinking, even in the medical establishment was that this was Nature's way.

One woman thought bigger than this. She launched a life-saving revolution and by the time she retired from the New York City Health Department in 1923 she was famous across the USA for having saved the lives of 90,000 inner city children and for implementing procedures that would save the lives of millions more around the world.

Her story is one of a big idea, of passionate interest, and going one step further.

When Sara Josephine Baker was studying to be a doctor she was fascinated with the health care of children and this became her passion and the focus of her career.

In 1902 Baker became a health inspector at New York's Department of Health and in her biography wrote that she 'climbed stair after stair, knocked on door after door, met drunk after drunk, filthy mother after filthy mother and dying baby after dying baby.'

Such a level of effort wasn't normal. As the New York Review of Books explained: 'Most of her fellow health inspectors didn't bother to make rounds at all; they just forged their records and went on their way.'

When she became the head of the newly formed Bureau of Child Hygiene she introduced preventative medicine. Instead of sick children being referred to physicians for consultations that might never happen or might happen too late to make a difference, she sent nurses to the single most 'deadly' neighbourhood in the Lower East Side with the job of meeting every new mother within a day of delivery.

The nurses job, said the Review, was 'encouraging exclusive breast-feeding, fresh air and regular bathing, and discouraging hazardous practices such as feeding the baby beer or allowing him to play in the gutter.'

This doesn't sounds like rocket science to us. But times change and like a trim tab these things can begin small so long as a good idea connects and people start sharing it. Making sure that every new mother learned the basics immediately she delivered a baby was thinking big and saving lives proved it. While the death rate remained stable in the other neighbourhoods, it actually fell in this, the worst neighbourhood of all.

The home-visiting programme was implemented across New York City alongside some other innovations such as setting up a network of 'milk stations' where babies were examined by doctors and milk formula was provided to mothers who couldn't breast feed.

'In just three years, the infant death rate in New York City fell by 40 per cent, and in December 1911, the New York Times hailed the city as the healthiest in the world.', said the New York Review of Books.

Don't wrestle the wind

When the current robust-looking competitive hot dog eating champs laugh at your puny frame and giant ambition don't be put off.

Once you start sharing your thinking you may well face criticism and resistance. Up with this you must just put. Climb back on your ride and keep going.

It is part of the process of thinking bigger.

If no-one's questioning you then you aren't doing anything new.

Resistance and criticism are inevitable parts of trying to think bigger.

And if you handle it right; if you think 'Yes and... ' accept the parts that are valid then this criticism will be like the sharpening stone that makes your blade finer not blunter.

Don't be weighted down by the criticism. And don't give up.

Work with it.

A yacht does not fight an opposing wind. It takes the wind's energy and it tacks to its destination.

Like a sailing boat your thoughts will tack toward the destination, indirectly.

That is the exploratory nature of all new ventures. If you went there directly then you were just copying someone-else's map and it's already been done so there's nothing new going on.

Making mistakes, acknowledging them, adjusting and continuing is how you make progress.

In sailing and in management speak it's called 'course correction'.

When you're working on your big idea you tack each time you take on board valid criticism.

Keep pitching; keep selling; keep thinking, keep telling your story til it's twanging.

And there's the sea squirt, clinging to a rock, waiting for things to happen. Every day is a Massive Monday of disappointment and compressed, beaten down dreams.

Meanwhile, overhead, your white horses surface and race across the brilliant blue.

You unfurl your sail and make the pursuit. You tack as the wind buffets you, all the while with your mind on the far, big horizon. Rarely is the chase direct, but life is an adventure after all (if you choose it to be).

Your sun rises.

Will you catch your white horse? Will you ride it back to shore?

Who knows?

But the chase is thrilling. And where your mind is, there you go.

This edition first published 2015
© 2015 Richard Newton

Registered office
John Wiley and Sons Ltd, The Atrium, Southern Gate, Chichester, West Sussex, PO19
8SQ, United Kingdom

For details of our global editorial offices, for customer services and for information
about how to apply for permission to reuse the copyright material in this book please
see our website at www.wiley.com.

Reprinted January 2015

Wiley publishes in a variety of print and electronic formats and by print-on-demand.
Some material included with standard print versions of this book may not be included in
e-books or in print-on-demand. If this book refers to media such as a CD or DVD that
is not included in the version you purchased, you may download this material at http://
booksupport.wiley.com. For more information about Wiley products, visit www.wiley.com.

Designations used by companies to distinguish their products are often claimed as
trademarks. All brand names and product names used in this book and on its cover
are trade names, service marks, trademark or registered trademarks of their respective
owners. The publisher and the book are not associated with any product or vendor
mentioned in this book. None of the companies referenced within the book have
endorsed the book.

Limit of Liability/Disclaimer of Warranty: While the publisher and author have used
their best efforts in preparing this book, they make no representations or warranties
with the respect to the accuracy or completeness of the contents of this book and
specifically disclaim any implied warranties of merchantability or fitness for a
particular purpose. It is sold on the understanding that the publisher is not engaged
in rendering professional services and neither the publisher nor the author shall be
liable for damages arising herefrom. If professional advice or other expert assistance is
required, the services of a competent professional should be sought.

A catalogue record for this book is available from the Library of Congress

A catalogue record for this book is available from the British Library.

ISBN 978-0-857-08585-6 (paperback)   ISBN 978-0-857-08587-0 (ebk)
ISBN 978-0-857-08588-7 (ebk)   ISBN 978-0-857-08586-3 (ebk)

Cover design/illustration: Rawshock Design

Internal pages designed by: Andy Prior Design Ltd

Set in Mendoza Roman Std, 9/11pt by Aptara, New Delhi, India
Printed in Great Britain by TJ International Ltd, Padstow, Cornwall, UK

IMAGE AND ILLUSTRATION LIST

P44 Traffic jam in Los Angeles – © egdigital/istockphoto.com

P48 Shed snakeskin © de-kay/istockphoto.com

P58 Ford Prefect, taken by Allen Watkin, Duxford, August 2009

P66 Statuette of laughing Buddha on a white background – © AlisLuch/istockphoto.com

P75 Tree of knowledge, sourced from http://upload.wikimedia.org/wikipedia/commons/c/c9/Arbor-scientiae.png

P84 Face on Mars, Viking 1 Orbiter, image F035A72 (Viking CD-ROM Volume 10), 25 July 1976

P127 Tornado on road – © andreusK/istockphoto.com

All other photos and illustrations by Richard Newton

ABOUT THE AUTHOR

 Richard Newton is an entrepreneur who writes.

Richard co-authored the best-selling book *Stop Talking Start Doing* which has been translated into 12 languages.

He is a co-founder of several technology businesses both in London, England and Austin, Texas. Many years before this, Richard was a business journalist for various Sunday newspapers in London.

He can be reached at www.richard-newton.com and @richnewton.

ACKNOWLEDGEMENTS

To everyone from Red Cottage but especially my parents without whose unflagging support and encouragement my mailing address would be somewhere in the Sargasso Sea.

And thanks to Holly, Jenny, Megan, Vicky, Sam and the amazing team at Capstone who brought this together at breakneck speed and showed that they do as they publish – anything is possible. Your timing was impeccable. More than you know.

READING LIST – A CHEAT SHEET FOR THINKING BIG

Like a pig in mud, I have bathed and rolled around in the inspiration, insights and words of many gifted thinkers and writers in putting together this book.

To list them all would consume a lot of space. Instead I'd like to point interested readers in the direction of some books, bloggers and idiosyncratic curators with whom spending some thinking time can only make your lives richer and your thinking bigger.

Blogs:
Maria Popova – brainpickings.com
Shane Parrish – farnamstreetblog.com
Tim Urban/Andrew Finn – waitbutwhy.com
Austin Kleon – austinkleon.com
Seth Godin – sethgodin.com
Daniel Pink – danpink.com
Tina Roth Eisenberg – swiss-miss.com
Cory Doctorow – boingboing.net
Ryan Holiday – ryanholiday.net
Tim Ferris – timferris.net

Books:
The Domesticated Brain – Bruce Hood
Operating Manual for Spaceship Earth – R. Buckminster Fuller
The Dude and the Zen Master – Jeff Bridges and Bernie Glassman
Bertrand Russell – In Praise of Idleness
The Element – Sir Ken Robinson
God Bless You Mister Rosewater – Kurt Vonnegut
Damn Good Advice for People with Talent – George Lois
Cultural Amnesia – Clive James

Amelia Earhart's white horse was a plane. She was the first woman to fly solo across the Atlantic.

> 'I flew the Atlantic because I wanted to. If that be what they call 'a woman's reason,' make the most of it. It isn't, I think, a reason to be apologized for by man or woman. . . .'

Whether you are flying the Atlantic or selling sausages or building a skyscraper or driving a truck, your greatest power comes from the fact that you want tremendously to do that very thing, and do it well.